AFRICAN ECONOMIC REFORM: THE EXTERNAL DIMENSION

Carol Lancaster

INSTITUTE FOR INTERNATIONAL ECONOMICS
WASHINGTON, DC
June 1991

Carol Lancaster is a Visiting Fellow at the Institute for International Economics and an Assistant Professor of Politics in the School of Foreign Service of Georgetown University. She was formerly a Deputy Assistant Secretary of State for African Affairs and a member of the Policy Planning Staff of the State Department. She is the author of numerous articles on foreign aid and on African politics and political economy, and coeditor (with John Williamson) of *African Debt and Financing*.

INSTITUTE FOR INTERNATIONAL ECONOMICS
11 Dupont Circle, NW
Washington, DC 20036
(202) 328-9000 Telex: 261271 IIE UR FAX: (202) 328-5432

Printed in the United States of America 93 92 91 3 2 1

Library of Congress Cataloging-in-Publication Data

Lancaster, Carol.
African economic reform : the external dimension / Carol Lancaster.
p. cm.—(Policy analyses in international economics; 33)
"June 1991."
Includes bibliographical references.
ISBN 0-88132-096-X: $12.95
1. Debts, External—Africa. 2. Debt relief—Africa. 3. Economic assistance—Africa. 4. Africa—Economic policy. I. Title. II. Series.
HJ8826.L36 1991 91-21933
336.3'436'096—dc20 CIP

Contents

TABLES

Preface

Africa continues to face the bleakest economic outlook of any region in the world. Its development prospects, exacerbated by its heavy external debt, are exceedingly poor. The problems of the continent thus remain high on the international agenda.

The Institute addressed these issues in 1986 in a Special Report entitled *African Debt and Financing,* based on a major conference held in Washington that brought together leading experts from Africa, the United States, and several other countries. This new study has been prepared by one of the coauthors of the 1986 report, Carol Lancaster, former Deputy Assistant Secretary of State for African Affairs and now on the faculty at Georgetown University, who is currently preparing a comprehensive study of foreign aid, diplomacy, and development in Africa for the Twentieth Century Fund. The present study updates the African economic problem, links its debt component to the overall need for external finance, relates that need in turn to the prospects for inducing the African countries to adopt required economic reforms, and proposes imaginative new institutional devices to achieve such a result. The Rockefeller Foundation provided financial support for the project.

The Institute for International Economics is a private nonprofit institution for the study and discussion of international economic policy. Its purpose is to analyze important issues in that area, and to develop and communicate practical new approaches for dealing with them. The Institute is completely nonpartisan.

The Institute was created by a generous commitment of funds from the German Marshall Fund of the United States in 1981 and now receives about 12 percent of its support from that source. In addition, major institutional grants are now being received from the Ford Foundation, the William and Flora Hewlett Foundation, the William M. Keck, Jr. Foundation, the Alfred P. Sloan Foundation, the C. V. Starr Foundation, and the United States–Japan Foundation. A number of other foundations and private corporations are contributing to the highly diversified financial resources of the Institute. About 15 percent of those resources in our latest fiscal year were provided by contributors outside the United States, including about 5 percent from Japan.

The Board of Directors bears overall responsibility for the Institute and gives general guidance and approval to its research program—including identification of topics that are likely to become important to international economic policymakers over the medium run (generally one to three years), and which thus should be addressed by the Institute. The Director, working closely with the staff and outside Advisory Committee, is responsible for the development of particular projects and makes the final decision to publish an individual study.

The Institute hopes that its studies and other activities will contribute to building a stronger foundation for international economic policy around the world. We invite readers of these publications to let us know how they think we can best accomplish this objective.

C. FRED BERGSTEN
Director
May 1991

Acknowledgments

The author is grateful for the many helpful comments and criticisms from those individuals who participated in the study group for this project, and to Jean-Claude Berthelemy, Richard N. Cooper and Robert S. Browne for their comments on the manuscript. The author wishes especially to thank C. Fred Bergsten, Catherine Gwin, Gerald Helleiner, Mamoudou Touré, and John Williamson, who were kind enough to read several versions of the manuscript and provide helpful comments on each, and John Underwood for his help in providing data and information. The views expressed in the manuscript are those of the author alone. Thanks are also due to the Institute's publications staff, and in particular Michael Treadway, for their editing as well as for their persistence, flexibility, and patience.

INSTITUTE FOR INTERNATIONAL ECONOMICS
11 Dupont Circle, NW, Washington, DC 20036-1207
(202) 328-9000 Telex: 261271 IIE UR FAX: (202) 328-5432

AFRICAN ECONOMIC REFORM: THE EXTERNAL DIMENSION

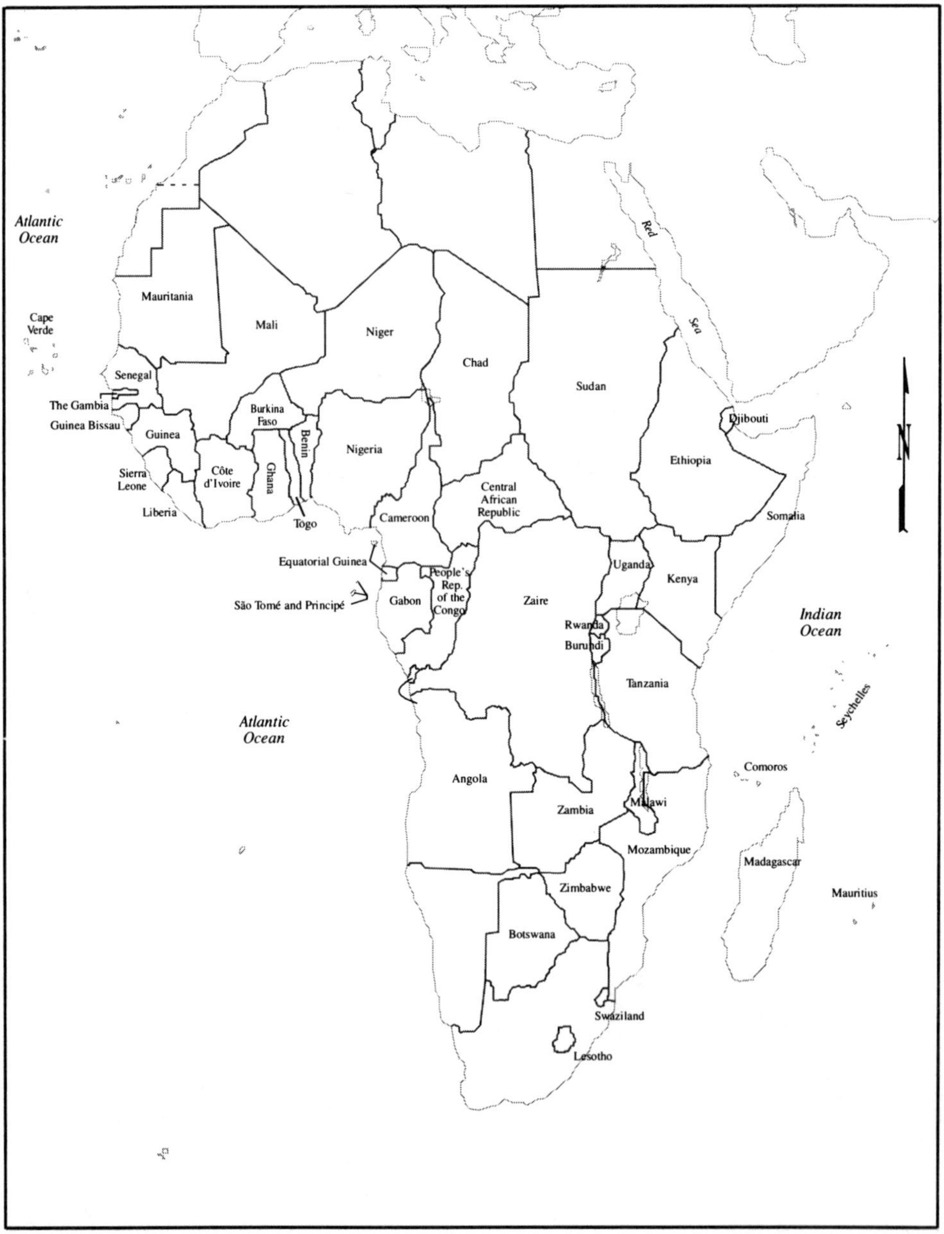

Adapted with permission from World Bank (1989).

1 The Development Challenge of Africa

Sub-Saharan Africa presents the world today with its most difficult development challenge. The 45 countries of Africa south of the Sahara include 32 that are classified by the World Bank as "low-income," with annual per capita incomes of $500 or less (see table A.1 in the appendix). These countries are among the poorest, least developed, and slowest growing in the world. Many of them also have some of the highest rates of population growth, some of the most exacting and fragile physical environments, and some of the least developed physical and human infrastructures in the world.

Even compared with India and China, most of Africa remains at a particularly early stage of development, with an average life expectancy at birth of 51 years, versus 58 for India and 70 for China.[1] The average population per physician is 24,000, compared with an average of 1,760 for China and India. In Africa only 73 percent of the eligible age group attend primary school, and only 20 percent are enrolled in secondary school. The corresponding percentages for China are 132 percent (this includes persons enrolled who are outside the conventional age group) and 43 percent, and for India 98 percent and 39 percent, respectively. A less tangible but no less important problem in Africa is the weakness and limited capacity of many public and private institutions; here again the Africans appear to compare unfavorably with India or China.

---

1. Except where otherwise indicated, "Africa" in this study refers to the countries of sub-Saharan Africa only, excluding Namibia and South Africa. The 45 countries that make up this group are listed in table A.1. The statistics in this study are drawn from World Bank publications. The three principal publications used are *Sub-Saharan Africa: From Crisis to Sustainable Growth* (World Bank 1989), *World Development Report* (World Bank 1990b), and *World Debt Tables 1990–91* (World Bank 1990a). Data on Namibia and South Africa are not included in these publications.

In addition to these low-income countries, seven African countries have average per capita incomes of between $500 and $1,000. The economies of these seven countries differ little from those of the lower-income countries. Indeed, some of them might well be classified as low-income if the currency (the CFA franc) shared by four of the seven were adjusted from its present exchange rate, widely regarded as overvalued, to an equilibrium rate. Several African countries formerly classified as middle-income—for example, Zambia and Nigeria—have recently been reclassified as low-income as their economic problems have worsened.

There are exceptions to this dismal economic picture. Botswana, a small, mineral-rich country with a history of good economic management, has achieved per capita income growth rates averaging between 7 percent and 10 percent per year. Cameroon and Mauritius have enjoyed per capita income growth rates of over 4 percent over much of the period since 1973. The Gambia, Malawi, Cape Verde, Swaziland, and Congo have regularly achieved average annual growth rates at least equal to their rates of population growth.

As at the time of their independence in the 1960s, African economies relied heavily on the production and export of a few primary products such as cocoa, coffee, cotton, sugar, peanuts, rubber, copper, phosphate, iron ore, or petroleum. In 1987, nearly 90 percent of African exports consisted of primary commodities, virtually the same proportion as in 1965.

With the earnings from these exports, plus whatever foreign aid and foreign credit they have access to, Africans must import much of their consumer durables, an increasing quantity of food, and nearly all of their intermediate and investment goods. Manufacturing as a proportion of their aggregate gross domestic product (GDP) was the same (10 percent) in 1987 as in 1965. Africa's experience with industrialization contrasts with that of other, more successful developing countries such as Korea, where manufacturing as a share of GDP rose from 18 percent in 1965 to 32 percent in 1988. Also unlike in Korea, manufactured goods produced in most African countries are rarely competitive internationally.

The reliance of African countries on the export of a few primary products has made their economies highly sensitive to conditions in those product markets. When the terms of trade for many African countries rose in the 1970s with the rise in prices of petroleum, metals, beverages, and some foodstuffs, many African governments suddenly found themselves with windfall foreign-exchange earnings. Rarely did they attempt to save their windfalls. Instead they spent them, often on expanded infrastructure or social services (which, although worthy in concept, did not generate revenues) or on poorly planned and often unproductive investments.

Some governments also borrowed against expected future export earnings. (This was a period, it will be remembered, when international banks were eager to lend surplus petrodollars.) In the latter half of the 1970s when, with the exception of oil, the prices of most primary-product prices fell, many African governments confronted a situation in which their imports, government employment, and expenditures had expanded while their export and budgetary revenues had dropped. The gaps in their external accounts and their government budgets were in part covered by additional aid, by additional commercial borrowing for those countries still enjoying access to bank credit, and, as time went on, by a compression in imports, which further depressed production, exports, export earnings, and investment.

Not surprisingly, over the past decade African countries have suffered from some of the slowest growth rates in the world. Per capita income was stagnant between 1973 and 1980 and fell by nearly 3 percent per year between 1981 and 1987. Growth rates improved in 1988 and 1989, with 14 countries enjoying growth in per capita income in 1988, and 15 in 1989. Only four had per capita income growth in 1981–84 (World Bank 1990c, 55). Contradicting the notion that positive per capita economic growth is simply impossible to sustain over several years in Africa, from 1965 to 1974 per capita incomes in the African countries rose by nearly 3 percent per year. But even with the positive growth rates of the earlier period, economic growth in Africa during much of the 1980s has been consistently below the average for low-income countries in other parts of the world. Moreover, having failed to diversify economically, African economies remain today largely within the narrow, rigid, and vulnerable productive bases they inherited at independence. As the Economic Commission for Africa (ECA) has emphasized repeatedly, Africans have failed to make the structural transformation associated with sustained growth.[2]

---

2. ECA (1989, 1). That report argues that the failure to transform the African economies is the cause of their current problems. It does not, however, explore why that failure occurred.

The Causes of Slow Development

What explains this poor development performance? The reasons differ from country to country but can be grouped into three categories. The first set of reasons relate to economic inheritance. Most African countries gained independence at a very early stage in their development, with limited human and physical infrastructure. In 1965, for example, only 40 percent of the relevant age group had access to primary education. The number of indigenous college graduates was minuscule. In Zaire it was thought to be fewer than 20 at independence. All-weather roads were few and typically ran from the interior to the coast and nowhere else. Similarly, communications systems linked African capitals to Europe but not to other cities within the country or to other capitals on the continent. The development challenges at independence were extensive, and many of the newly independent countries had a limited capacity to deal with them. In surveying the many development challenges facing Ghana at independence, Kwame Nkrumah, that country's first president, borrowed a lament from Tennyson: "So much to do, so little done. . . ." (Nkrumah 1970).

It is no surprise, then, that many African governments were in a hurry to promote their countries' development. Their understandable haste, however, contributed to a second set of factors underlying Africa's poor economic performance: the accumulated problems of economic mismanagement by African leaders. A combination of the weak capacity of many governments (including a lack of economic expertise, poor organization and training of government officials, too many and conflicting objectives imposed on particular agencies or institutions, and poor leadership), the overriding political goals of leaders, and the tendency of many African politicians and bureaucrats to regulate as much of their economies as was feasible has resulted in a litany of economic woes. By the 1980s, many of these countries suffered from bloated and inefficient bureaucracies; controlled prices, wages, and interest rates, which have distorted economic signals and depressed productive sectors; and overvalued currencies, which have depressed the production of agricultural and other tradeable goods and exacerbated trade deficits. All of these ills, together with controls on trade, have led to thriving black markets and widespread smuggling, and have fed the inevitable tendencies on the part of public officials and the public alike toward rent seeking and corruption.

The third category of causes behind the deepening economic crisis in sub-Saharan Africa is the sharp deterioration in the region's terms of trade from the historic highs during the early 1980s. This decline, described above, forced a compression in imports and hit the poorer, oil-importing countries especially hard. The cutback in imports resulted in a drop in domestic production and exports and another turn in the downward economic spiral.

Rapid population growth has complicated this welter of economic problems and heightened the urgency of resolving them. Since independence, population growth has been accelerating rapidly in Africa, from 2.6 percent per year between 1965 and 1973 to 2.8 percent per year between 1973 and 1980, finally reaching 3.1 percent per year since 1980. These rates are historically unprecedented.[3] Developing countries in other regions of the world today typically have population growth rates below 3 percent, and those rates are declining.

Accelerating rates of population growth in Africa are, ironically, a result of successful past development: Africa has largely completed the first stage of the so-called demographic transition, as improved hygiene, medical services, and nutrition have brought down both overall death rates and childhood mortality rates. But unlike other parts of the developing world, Africa has not yet entered the second stage of that transition, in which fertility rates also decline as families begin to limit the number of live births to achieve their desired family size. Indeed, fertility rates in low-income Africa have risen over the past two decades.[4]

---

3. Except where population growth has been fed through immigration, as in the case of the United States during periods in the 19th century.

4. There is some evidence that fertility rates in several African countries are beginning to decline (van de Walle and Foster 1990, 5–11). But this evidence remains preliminary and thus far too weak on which to base projections or conclusions. Also uncertain is the probable impact of AIDS on child survival rates.

Although there is little agreement among experts on why fertility continues to rise in Africa, it is quite likely that deepening poverty plays a significant role. The pressures on African families to reproduce are economic as well as social: more children promise greater security in old age and may provide rural families with a claim on a larger allocation of communal land. Where they do not have access to school and can instead help in the fields and in the home, children are regarded as providing net economic benefits. As long as children bring such benefits, and as long as women lack the education that usually accompanies a desire for smaller families, or lack the resources to acquire birth control devices, Africa will continue to produce large numbers of children.

World Bank projections of the future population of Africa are alarming. From a base of 450 million in 1987, the African population is projected to increase to nearly 670 million by 2000 and to 1.3 billion by 2025. By that year, the population of Africa will be just under that of India (at 1.4 billion) and China (at 1.5 billion), and Nigeria will be the third-largest developing country in the world, with a population of 286 million (compared with estimates of just over 110 million today).

The impact of the AIDS epidemic in East, Central, Southern, and parts of West Africa on population growth rates is as yet unclear. It could reduce these growth rates in countries where the infection is widespread. So far, however, the death rate from AIDS is not projected to be high enough to have a major impact on overall population growth rates.

Such rapid population growth makes future development in Africa an especially difficult challenge. The region must grow at rates considerably above those of the last several decades just to stay in the same place economically. Rapidly growing populations, the majority of which are likely to remain in rural areas, put increasing pressures on fragile environments. Indeed, expanding populations are already depressing agricultural productivity in a number of countries. Although fertile, unexploited agricultural land exists in a few of the poor countries of Africa, such as Sudan, in many countries an arid climate, uncertain rainfall, variable and fragile soils, and unconquered pests and diseases are far more typical.

To increase food production to keep up with population growth and to avoid environmental degradation, Africans must develop, adapt, and implement technological improvements in agricultural production and land conservation. The dramatic production increases associated with the Green Revolution in other parts of the developing world do not appear likely in Africa in the foreseeable future. The high-yielding varieties of wheat and rice that permitted a major expansion in food production in India, Indonesia, and Latin America cannot be used in Africa because of the different climates, soil conditions, and pests there, and because most farmers lack access to irrigation and fertilizers.

Rapid population growth puts great pressure not only on land but on cities as well. The flood of Africans moving to urban areas produces a burgeoning labor force looking for jobs in the modern sector of the economy. The rate of urbanization in sub-Saharan Africa averaged 5.5 percent to 5.7 percent per year during the period from 1965 to 1980; it accelerated to 7 percent per year in the 1980s. The failure of metropolitan governments to keep up with the rapidly rising demand for services, and the failure of the manufacturing and service sectors to expand to absorb the influx, have already produced in some African cities the slums and unemployment already familiar in India and parts of Latin America. One can only surmise what African cities and employment pressures will be like in the next century if economic growth and industry fail to expand with the population.

A particularly troubling trend is the growing number of African countries torn by internal strife: Chad and Uganda in the recent past; Liberia, Somalia, Sudan, Ethiopia, Mozambique, Angola, and, increasingly, South Africa at present. Although many different factors have fed these various conflicts, they appear to share one common pattern: they erupt between ethnically distinct groups (or distinct clans, as in the case of Somalia), as those groups that find themselves excluded from power, repressed, exploited, or dominated challenge those in power. African states are artifacts of the colonial period, when borders were drawn to suit the convenience of the colonial powers, not to reflect demographic or geographic reality; hence there are few without ethnic, religious, racial, or religious cleavages. The growing number of internal conflicts underlines the complex and difficult problems confronting African politicians of how to manage national diversity. These problems are made all the more challenging by economic distress, and in turn the conflicts have been economically devastating to the countries where they have occurred. In the Horn of Africa, armed conflict has combined with a serious drought to raise the specter of starvation on a massive scale, possibly affecting as many as 15 million people.

The Role of Aid

The 32 countries of low-income Africa in particular, with the exception of Nigeria, have become heavily dependent on foreign aid (see table A.2 in the appendix).[5] Almost from the moment of independence, most African governments actively sought and received substantial amounts of aid relative to the size of their economies. Concessional assistance now exceeds 15 percent of GNP in nearly half of Africa's poorer countries (and is much higher in several). Even more striking is the fact that two-thirds of imports and as much as 100 percent of the investment in low-income Africa are financed with foreign aid. There are few historical precedents for a group of independent countries relying so heavily on foreign subsidies over a period of a decade or more.

One implication of this dependence on aid is that, without its continuation in substantial amounts, consumption, production, and investment in these countries would drop precipitously. Such a drop in countries as poor as many in Africa could cause considerable human suffering. Another implication is that providing such large amounts of aid puts considerable leverage in the donors' hands, as well as responsibility for what happens economically in the aid-dependent countries.

Despite the relatively high levels of aid to Africa over the decades, the results of aid there are among the most disappointing of any part of

---

5. Nigeria is an outlier in this regard, with foreign aid equal to less than 1 percent of the country's GNP. Because of its size and abundant revenues from petroleum during the 1970s, many aid donors reduced or discontinued their assistance to Nigeria. They are only now beginning to resume aid programs there in the wake of prolonged economic decline.

the world, with rates of project failure among the highest anywhere.[6] There are a number of reasons for this unhappy record. In addition to the problems of poor economic management, already described, too many governments and international institutions have provided aid for diverse and at times contradictory purposes. Some, like the United States, have deployed their aid in support of geopolitical objectives regardless of the nature of the recipient government. For example, the government of Zaire, with one of the worst development records in the world, has been the largest single recipient of American aid in sub-Saharan Africa since the United States began providing aid to the region in the late 1950s. That aid was driven primarily by political motives, including the desire to strengthen the government against internal and external threats and to deny the Soviet Union the opportunity to gain influence in one of Africa's largest, most strategically located, and potentially richest countries. In 1990, US political interests having diminished sharply with the end of the Cold War, Congress finally mandated a termination of US economic assistance to the government of Zaire, and the administration acquiesced.

Other aid donors, such as the Italians and at times the French, have used their aid to promote their commercial exports regardless of the price, productivity, or priority of those exports for African development needs. Even where aid-giving agencies have had support of African development as their primary goal, the effectiveness of aid has frequently been disappointing, with donors promoting different visions of development, and different and at times inappropriate types of projects requiring diverse and nonsubstitutable equipment. In short, aid-giving institutions have too seldom coordinated what they have actually financed in Africa, despite their many discussions of aid coordination, and too often they have acted irresponsibly. The Africans themselves, eager for aid and often lacking the capacity (or willingness) to reject it or to shape it to promote their own development, have compounded the

6. See, for example, World Bank (1988, 1990d) and other World Bank assessments of the effectiveness of its lending operations. AID evaluations of its lending operations in Africa generally echo the experience of the Bank (see the agency's various Project Impact Evaluation Reports on Africa).

problem of waste and ineffectiveness. The problem of aid dependence is likely to continue and even increase, with the Africans and their aid donors remaining hostage to one another—hardly the basis for a healthy relationship on either side.

The Experiment in Economic Reform

The increasingly serious economic problems plaguing Africa at the end of the 1970s and the beginning of the 1980s provoked a reexamination of the causes of Africa's economic problems and their potential solutions. A major study published by the World Bank in 1981, titled *Accelerated Development in Sub-Saharan Africa,* focused world attention on the policy failures of African governments and on the need for fundamental economic reforms. Adding to the arguments made in the World Bank study and elsewhere were the growing pressures on African governments from developed-country governments and the international financial institutions (IFIs) to undertake reform programs. The decade of the 1980s in Africa has been marked by efforts on the part of an ever-expanding number of African governments to implement economic reforms. During this time, developed-country governments and the IFIs have conditioned an increasing proportion of their aid on the adoption by the Africans of acceptable stabilization and structural adjustment programs. Programs of stabilization and structural adjustment in sub-Saharan Africa[7] were almost always initiated as a result of the African government's desperation for foreign exchange and debt relief, combined with pressures and threats from developed-country governments that no debts would be rescheduled, that no additional aid would be forthcoming, and that existing aid levels could be cut if acceptable reforms were not implemented.

External agencies have played an important role not just in the initiation but also in the maintenance of reforms in Africa. A principal reason for this is one peculiar to African societies: the beneficiaries of reforms are weak politically (the farmers) or are very limited in number (the

---

7. See, for example, Gulhati (1989a and b), Calleghy (1990), McPherson and Radelet (1989), and Berg (1990).

large-scale private entrepreneurs). At the same time, those whose interests are typically hurt by reform programs—civil servants and other urban workers and elites who enjoy rents from existing economic policies or secure jobs in the modern sector—are among the most powerful elements in African societies. They can resist or reverse reforms once the sense of economic crisis abates or external pressures for reforms ease. The weakness of the proreform constituency in African societies makes it particularly important that external pressures for reforms are sustained until they are effective in achieving sustainable growth and in creating a constituency influential enough to protect them.

For external agencies to be effective in promoting economic reform in sub-Saharan Africa, they must also be consistent in their policy advice. Where IFIs and foreign governments have differed on the importance or shape of reform programs, African officials have managed to play them off against one another to avoid implementing painful stabilization or adjustment policies. In the case of Zaire during part of the 1980s a pattern became evident in which the Zairian government would promise reforms, receive external financing based on that promise, and then ignore the reform commitments or reverse some of the reforms actually implemented. It would then negotiate new reform programs, beginning the pattern over again. This pattern was a direct result of President Mobutu Sese Seko's influence in Washington, Brussels, and Paris (and occasionally elsewhere) and his ability to manipulate that influence to his advantage. The case of Zaire is the most blatant but far from the only example of a strategy on the part of Africans of avoiding reforms by enlisting the support of foreign patrons and playing them off against one another.

There is another reason why it is important that the IFIs and foreign governments continue to urge and finance reform programs in Africa. The capacity of African governments to shape reform programs is limited. Senior African economic officials often are highly qualified professionals but lack the depth of staff capacity necessary to deal adequately with the myriad economic issues confronting them daily. The IFIs in particular can provide critical support in the form of advice, technical assistance, and training,[8] but to do so they must remain

8. A new World Bank initiative is just getting under way to support an expansion in the opportunities for young African economists and managers to obtain the training and

actively engaged and focused on promoting adjustment, and they must retain the support of the developed-country governments. The weak administrative capacity of African governments further underlines the importance of consistent policy advice from external institutions on adjustment. When that advice is not consistent or well coordinated, or is simply too extensive, it imposes an unfair burden on those already overtaxed African officials charged with implementing economic reforms in their countries.

During the 1980s, confronted with worsening economic problems, African governments began to implement programs of economic restructuring: stabilization programs, usually supported by the IMF, aimed at reducing the gap in their balance of payments, and structural adjustment programs, supported by the World Bank and foreign aid donors, intended to improve the efficiency of national economic resources and encourage additional production and private investment. The Bretton Woods institutions—the IMF and the World Bank—have become the lead agencies in advising, pressuring, financing, and monitoring economic restructuring programs in sub-Saharan Africa. They are generally supported by developed-country governments in this role, and increasingly those governments are cofinancing structural adjustment programs with the World Bank. (One senior World Bank official recently estimated that, of the $15 billion in concessional assistance flowing to Africa, $12 billion was now associated with World Bank–approved structural adjustment programs.) Over 30 African countries are currently engaged in or have recently implemented programs of stabilization, structural adjustment, or both.

The general strategy behind programs of economic restructuring is seldom explicitly described but nevertheless widely shared by officials in the Bretton Woods institutions, in the US government and in other

---

experience that will help them better advise their own governments on economic policy choices in the future, as well as manage that policy effectively. The African Capacity Building Initiative will provide training and fellowships to Africans, create regional institutions to provide training in economic analysis and management, create economic policy units within African governments, and attempt to strengthen existing capacities within African governments for economic policy analysis and implementation.

donor governments, and increasingly by African economic managers as well. It assumes that Africans, despite their cultural, political, or economic differences vis-à-vis the developed countries, will respond to economic incentives in predictable ways. Like individuals elsewhere, they will eventually expand their production and investment where they can earn increased income and profits. "Structural" obstacles—cultural values, limited physical infrastructure, vested political interests—may delay but will not prevent such a response. Thus, with appropriate incentives in terms of prices and other market signals, production will eventually expand and investment increase in adjusting countries.

Implicit in this approach appears to be the assumption, based on past history, that African governments lack the capabilities to identify and implement effective state-led growth strategies. The thrust of the Bretton Woods institutions' strategy has been increasingly to reduce the role of government in economic management through freeing up prices, wages, and interest rates; eliminating subsidies; liberalizing trade; adjusting currencies to reflect market conditions; reducing the number and influence of state-owned enterprises; and shaping investment codes to promote hoped-for private investment.[9] Investment (domestic and foreign) in agriculture or industry is expected to occur in response to new opportunities in Africa and, in effect, become an engine of future growth. Meanwhile, external financing is needed to pay for the imports required to increase utilization of existing capacity, to maintain and expand public investments such as infrastructure, and to increase the availability of consumer durables.

It appears from World Bank analyses that overall economic growth, growth in the volume of exports, and growth in gross domestic saving have all been consistently higher in those countries undertaking strong

---

9. Not everyone agrees with this assumption. The ECA published a report in 1989 challenging the effectiveness of IMF- and World Bank-supported economic reforms in Africa and arguing for a greater role for the state in managing African economies. At the same time, the ECA recognized that, in the past, African governments had proved to be poor economic managers. It did not explain why these governments would be any better in the future than they had been in the past.

TABLE 1 GDP growth rates in four reforming African countries, 1981–89 (percentages)[a]

Country	1981–84	1985–87	1988–89
Ghana	−2.3	4.7	5.9
Madagascar	1.6	1.8	3.9
Malawi	1.8	1.8	3.5
Togo	−3.0	3.0	4.7

a. Annual averages.
Source: World Bank (1990b, 13).

reform programs than in those whose reforms were less comprehensive or intense. In Ghana, Malawi, Togo, and Madagascar, where reform programs have been under way the longest, average growth rates for the period 1988–89 are well above those prevailing in those countries in the early or mid–1980s, before or shortly after adjustment programs were implemented (table 1).[10] This turnaround in the growth statistics is likely to be the result of more favorable weather and rising levels of aid as well as of the reforms. But the contrast between the strong reformers and those whose programs were less comprehensive or sustained is unmistakable, as is that between the performance of the

10. "Strong" reformers by the World Bank's (1990, 13) criteria include Burundi, the Gambia, Ghana, Kenya, Madagascar, Malawi, and Togo. "Average" performers include the Central African Republic, Chad, Guinea, Guinea-Bissau, Mali, Mozambique, Sao Tome and Principe, Senegal, Tanzania, and Uganda. "Weak" performers include Benin, Mauritania, Niger, Somalia, and Zaire. Interestingly, the World Bank's statistics for 1988 and 1989 show higher rates of real domestic investment in average and weak performers than in strong performers. This may reflect more stringent policies regarding credit creation and government expenditures in those countries.

The ECA (1989) has claimed that countries undertaking strong reform programs have suffered from the poorest economic performance. But the ECA bases that argument on statistics averaged over the entire decade of the 1980s; this obscures the impact of the adjustment programs, most of which commenced at the middle of the decade. Also, the ECA's statistical series end in 1987, when many of the "strong" reform programs were just getting under way.

reforming countries before and after their reforms. This suggests that the reforms have begun to produce results. A study by John Williamson (1990) also found that most of a sample of Latin American countries implementing strong reform programs over several years enjoyed greater improvements in growth rates than those that did not.

Even though much of the region is now engaged in economic restructuring programs, with some positive signs of economic recovery in evidence, new private investment, so important for renewed growth and to decrease reliance on aid, remains extremely small. Why has this new private investment not been forthcoming, even from Africans who are believed to hold considerable amounts of capital outside their countries? There is an emerging consensus on the answer to this question, at least in Washington. First, among some African leaders and among many middle-level African bureaucrats there is still suspicion and hostility toward the private sector, above all toward foreign private capital and private entrepreneurs of non-African origin—Asians in East and Southern Africa, Lebanese in West Africa. The fear of continuing outside control of their countries and economies, combined with the rhetoric of socialism and sometimes the reality as well, characterized the first two decades of independence throughout much of the region. For many years, capitalism was identified with colonialism by Africans who rejected both. Many Africans are finding it hard to shed the beliefs learned during the 1960s and 1970s.

A second obstacle to foreign investment is an oppressive bureaucracy. Extensive, expensive, and time-consuming red tape in many countries still discourages all but the most committed investors. For foreign investors the red tape and even harassment often begin as soon as they arrive at an African airport. The problems of dealing with local officials are often compounded by inadequate and unreliable transport and communications facilities and, in some countries, uncertain electricity flows.

Third, even where government statements welcoming private investment are sincere, there is often a more difficult problem. Political power is still highly centralized in most of Africa and is at times used by leaders and bureaucrats in arbitrary ways for their political or personal benefit. The issue is one of more than petty corruption or even insecure property rights, which are also problems in other parts of the world (see Williamson 1990). It involves the arbitrary and capricious implementation of laws and regulations, the lack of due process, and in some places a complete absence of the rule of law.

Added to these problems are the political changes taking place in much of Africa today: under pressure from disgruntled populations, some of Africa's autocrats have began to implement political reforms, permitting multiple political parties, elections, and greater freedom for the media. It is as yet unclear how far these changes will go in moving African countries toward more open, democratic political systems, how long they will be sustained, or what their effect on African economic performance will be. The changes may prove ephemeral, lasting only as long as the ruling politicians find them necessary to quiet domestic discontent or to respond to external pressures for democratization. Even if they endure, they could slow or even reverse economic reforms as politicians focus their attention and energies on retaining (or gaining) power. On the other hand, if the reforms are consolidated, they could produce more open, responsible governments. Understandably, businesspeople are reluctant at present to risk their capital in such circumstances, even when there are opportunities to make profits. They usually have far better, less risky investment alternatives in other parts of the world.

The lack of investor response to new opportunities in Africa presents the Bretton Woods institutions, the developed-country governments supporting them, and the African governments implementing economic reforms with a serious dilemma. The problems inhibiting new investment in Africa are less problems of economic policy than problems with the behavior of public officials—in short, of governance. These are essentially political problems and cannot easily be handled by aid agencies with existing instruments of economic restructuring. Both the ECA and the World Bank have explicitly pointed to the problems of governance in Africa in their most recent reports on the region, and these problems have been further emphasized in recent publications by the World Bank and speeches by its president and other officials.

However, having identified the problem, World Bank officials are still struggling internally to understand the nature and causes of poor governance in Africa and what the Bank and other external agencies can do about it. The Bank has pointed to several conditions associated with poor governance, namely, the lack of public accountability, probity, transparency, consistency, and predictability. But these conditions have existed in other countries and have resulted neither in poor governance nor in poor economic performance. And in at least one democratic country in Africa, the Gambia, a measure of transparency and public accountability has failed to ensure good economic performance. These conditions by themselves do not explain why governance in so many African societies has been poor.

The root causes of poor governance in Africa have been linked variously to historical, cultural, social, and political factors. Some see it as a natural outgrowth of communal values and obligations, which continue to exert a strong influence on Africans, including those in public positions who are expected to use their positions to benefit their relatives or clansmen. Other observers attribute it to the autocratic political structures typical of African countries where the behavior of public officials has rarely been subject to public scrutiny or criticism. Still others have focused on political institutions, such as the absence of an independent judiciary, a free press, multiple political parties, or free elections, as sources of poor governance. There is as yet little consensus on the fundamental factors affecting governance in Africa.

What to do about poor governance presents external financing agencies with a difficult dilemma. The quality of governance is important to the success of economic reforms. However, addressing governance problems in Africa may lead external financing agencies to add political reforms to their agenda for change in Africa. This could be highly intrusive. The challenge of the 1990s will be to understand better the root causes of poor governance in Africa and identify what external agencies can do to help improve it without exceeding either their mandates or their capacities.

Meanwhile, the task of supporting economic reform in Africa today is to address not only the obstacles to effective reform but also to ensure that reforms are adequately financed. It is to the issue of African financing needs that we now turn.

2 Financing African Reforms

For economic reforms in Africa to be effective in stimulating recovery and sustained growth, Africans must be able to import the raw materials, spare parts, investment goods, and consumption goods they need to expand their production, income, and exports. With the deterioration in their terms of trade and decreases in domestic economic activity, most African countries have produced and exported less, not more, over the past decade. This is in large part a result of import strangulation. External financing is essential in relieving this import constraint. But how much external financing is needed?

Africa's Resource Needs

Estimating the resource needs of developing countries is still more of an art than a science. In its simplest form, it typically involves identification of a target rate of growth, estimating the quantity of investment needed to achieve that target (this estimate, in turn, must be based on an estimate of the efficiency of investment), and projecting the amount of domestically generated savings available for investment, including earnings from exports. The gaps between domestic savings and investment and between export earnings and import needs required to achieve the growth target must be filled with a mix of foreign aid, debt relief, foreign private investment, and commercial borrowing from abroad. For much of Africa, foreign private investment and foreign commercial borrowing are extremely limited and appear likely to remain so for the immediate future. External financing must come primarily from aid and debt relief.

The World Bank, in its most recent study on Africa's economic problems and prospects, entitled *Sub-Saharan Africa: From Crisis to Sustainable Growth* (World Bank 1989), attempted to estimate needs and debt relief for the region during the 1990s. Assuming an initial target of 4 percent growth per year, increasing to 5 percent by 2000, the Bank projects needed increases in concessional assistance averaging 4 percent per year during the 1990s, with total aid to Africa rising from $15 billion in 1990 to $22 billion by the year 2000. (The $22 billion figure is based on 1990 prices. Inflation would increase in nominal terms the total amount needed for the year 2000.) In addition, the Bank projects the need for sufficient debt relief to keep actual debt-servicing payments from exceeding their present real level ($9 billion per year for all of sub-Saharan Africa) and an inflow of annual nonconcessional borrowings, new foreign direct investment, and net private transfers at the same $6 billion level they estimate it has averaged over the past decade. There are trade-offs among these resources. For example, to the extent that foreign aid falls short of these goals, debt relief would have to increase if overall growth targets are to be met, and vice versa. Likewise an increase in the growth target by 1 percent per year would require an increase in aid, debt relief, or other external financing of 20 percent to 25 percent, or roughly $6 billion to $7 billion (Culagovski et al. 1990, 22).

There are three troubling elements in the Bank's scenario, all of which suggest that the Bank may have underestimated the region's likely need for external financing over the coming decade. First, the Bank's target rates of growth are low. Growth rates of 4 percent or 5 percent per year over the decade would barely stay ahead of population increases (expected to average 3 percent per year). This rate of growth would permit only a very limited increase in consumption during the 1990s, as the expansion of income over population growth would be allocated largely to investment. Disaggregating the forecast income and consumption figures, the Bank projects that the poorer segments of African society may enjoy a small increase in consumption while the better-off segments see their consumption fall further. It must be asked whether this scenario is politically sustainable after a decade and a half of economic decline, and particularly whether the assumption that African elites will tolerate a continuing contraction in their incomes for another decade is realistic.

Some have speculated as to why the Bank's growth targets have been so modest. For example, Gerald Helleiner of the University of Toronto has suggested that "...the World Bank has consistently understated

Africa's medium-term requirements so as to generate aid targets which the major industrialized countries would consider within the range they consider to be politically possible" (Helleiner 1991, 5). Bank staff confirm privately that "realism" about what levels of concessional aid are expected to be available plays a role in their calculations of financing gaps and growth targets.

Second, some of the assumptions about economic conditions in African countries appear heroic. Domestic saving, investment, the efficiency of investment, and exports are all assumed to rise significantly over levels prevailing during the 1980s. None of these assumptions is impossible to realize, but the likelihood of all of them being achieved over the coming decade would appear small. Investment as a proportion of GNP and the efficiency of investment by the year 2000 are assumed to exceed the levels achieved over the past decade and a half. To the extent that African economies fail to achieve any one of these goals, either their rate of growth will be smaller than the target or they will require additional external financing.

Third, in addressing the needs of sub-Saharan Africa for concessional aid over the coming decade, the Bank suggests that an increase of 4 percent in real terms per year is a realistic expectation. Concessional aid to sub-Saharan Africa has increased by more than this amount annually over the past 10 years. But the 1990s could well prove quite different, with much more modest increases in Japanese and Italian aid than were seen during the 1980s. Indeed, a decline in Italian bilateral aid to Africa was already evident by the end of the 1980s. A stagnation or even a decline in US aid also appears possible, as does a diversion in aid from Western European countries to Eastern Europe and, temporarily, to the Middle East in the wake of the war in the Persian Gulf.[1] There are also the needs for additional aid on the part of politically and

1. US bilateral economic assistance to Africa, after declining for several years, rose in 1991 as Congress appropriated more than the administration requested. It remains to be seen whether the Black Caucus, which was the principal force behind the increase, will continue to press for and obtain such increases in the future. For more details see Lancaster (1991).

economically liberalizing Latin American governments; the needs for assistance to South American coca-producing countries if sufficient incentives are ever provided to their coca growers to shift to other crops; the needs for increased assistance among the poorer Asian countries, the politically troubled Philippines and poverty-stricken Bangladesh in particular; and the needs, occasionally very large, for aid to relieve natural and man-made catastrophes, as in Bangladesh, Iraq, and the Horn of Africa.

Combined with rising needs abroad for external financing are continuing budgetary stringencies in major aid-giving countries, including the United States, the United Kingdom, and Italy. The list is likely to extend to the Federal Republic of Germany as it absorbs the former East Germany, and possibly to Japan if the yen continues to decline. Economic aid from Arab oil producers has already dropped, and economic assistance from Eastern Europe and the Soviet Union, already small in most African countries, is likely to vanish altogether as well, as the new governments in these countries rethink their foreign policies and begin to address their pressing domestic needs. In short, there is no assurance that concessional assistance for Africa will rise in the 1990s at the rates at which it rose in the 1980s; indeed, there is even a possibility that it could decline. With African financing needs growing and external resources available for financing possibly stagnating or declining, the importance of additional debt relief measures takes on increased urgency.

A Profile of African Debt

In 1989, the 45 countries of sub-Saharan Africa owed a total of $147 billion to foreign governments, private lenders, and IFIs (see table A.3 in the appendix). For some African countries, the stock of debt and the servicing of that debt were manageable. But for many low-income and a handful of middle-income African countries, the burden of external debt was severe. It is on these troubled countries that we shall focus our analysis of African debt.

There are at present in Africa 24 severely indebted low-income countries and 3 severely indebted middle-income countries.[2] The total debt of the severely indebted countries of low-income Africa amounted to $102 billion in 1989.[3] Nearly a third of this total, or $32 billion, is owed by Nigeria. In examining the components of low-income African debt, it is important to look at Nigeria's debt separately, since it has a profile different from the debt of the rest of low-income Africa.

SEVERELY INDEBTED LOW-INCOME AFRICA (EXCEPT NIGERIA)

The 23 severely indebted low-income African countries had a total external debt of $68 billion in 1989: $30 billion was owed to foreign governments, $22 billion to multilateral institutions such as the World Bank and the IMF, $7 billion to private creditors on medium- and long-term credits, and $9 billion in part to private creditors in payment for short-term loans and in part in arrears.

The value or stock of debt of these countries was equal to 106 percent of the total value of their goods and services in 1989—the highest ratio of debt to GNP of any major grouping of debtor nations in the world. Debt–GNP ratios for Mexico and Brazil, for comparison, were 51 per-

---

2. The 24 severely indebted low-income African countries are the following: Benin, Burundi, Comoros, Equatorial Guinea, Ghana, Guinea, Guinea-Bissau, Kenya, Liberia, Madagascar, Malawi, Mali, Mauritania, Mozambique, Niger, Nigeria, Sao Tome and Principe, Sierra Leone, Somalia, Sudan, Tanzania, Togo, Zaire, and Zambia. The severely indebted middle-income African countries include Congo, Cote d'Ivoire, and Senegal. The World Bank classifies countries as severely indebted if three of four key debt ratios are above critical levels. These ratios and their critical levels are as follows: the debt–GNP ratio, 50 percent or higher; debt to exports of goods and services (the debt-export ratio), 275 percent or higher; the ratio of accrued debt-servicing obligations to exports (the debt service ratio), 30 percent or higher; and the ratio of accrued interest to exports, 20 percent or higher. There are in all 26 severely indebted low-income countries and 20 severely indebted middle-income countries in the world.

3. At the time of this writing the 1990 figures were projections, with many details still lacking.

cent and 24 percent, respectively. Specialists in problems of external debt generally consider a debt–GNP ratio of more than 40 percent as likely to indicate a serious economic problem.[4]

Another important aspect of a country's debt is the amount of resources actually paid out each year to service the debt. Debt servicing by the severely indebted low-income African countries (still excluding Nigeria) in 1989 totaled $3 billion. Nearly two-thirds of these payments went to multilateral institutions: $1.1 billion, or a third, was paid to the IMF alone. Another 20 percent ($600 million) was paid to private creditors. The remaining 16 percent, or $500 million, went to service debts to foreign governments.

It is important to note that whereas the 23 low-income African countries considered here actually paid $3 billion to service their debt in 1989, they were scheduled to pay more than $6 billion. A combination of debt reschedulings, debt cancellations, and accumulation of arrears resulted in their actual debt servicing equaling only half of their scheduled servicing.

It is also worth noting that whereas half of the debt of the severely indebted low-income African countries was owed to foreign governments, a far smaller proportion of their actual debt servicing—only 16 percent—was actually paid to those governments. On the other hand, only one-third of their total debt was owed to multilateral financial

---

4. See Williamson (1991, forthcoming) and Green (1989). Although a debt–GNP ratio of over 100 percent is a sign of a particularly heavy debt burden, one important caveat needs to be made. Figures on debt stocks are aggregates. They are not yet sufficiently refined to indicate the degree of concessionality or the present value of that debt, and so may overestimate the real burden of a stock of debt that includes a high proportion of concessional credits. For example, a government with $100 million in debt obtained on hard terms (commercial rates of interest, short- to medium-term maturities) must transfer a larger amount of real resources to retire that debt than a government with $100 million in debt borrowed on soft terms (below-market rates of interest, long grace and repayment periods). For this group of low-income African governments, a significant proportion of whose debts are in the form of concessional loans from the World Bank, the African Development Fund, and developed-country governments, the debt–GNP ratio is likely to exaggerate the debt burden somewhat compared with the debt burdens of better-off countries with larger proportions of commercial credits. But even with this caveat, there is no doubt that the debt burden of severely indebted low-income Africa is a heavy one.

institutions, but two-thirds of their debt repayments went to these organizations. There are two principal reasons for these apparent anomalies: the fact that the IFIs—unlike governments—do not reschedule their debts, and the high costs associated with a failure on the part of borrowers to service debts to these institutions. Since their creation, the World Bank, the IMF, and other multilateral lending institutions modeled on them have been preferred lenders. The World Bank and the regional development banks do not reschedule their debts on the grounds that their ratings in world credit markets (from which they obtain a substantial proportion of their financing) would be damaged, either reducing their access to those markets or increasing their cost of borrowing.

Where governments borrowing from IFIs fail to service their loans in a timely fashion, access to new lending from these institutions is eventually cut off. A cutoff of IFI lending is seen by commercial and bilateral public lenders as a sign of a serious lack of financial responsibility on the part of the creditor government and usually results in a loss of access to commercial credits (including short-term trade credits), government-guaranteed or -financed export credits, and, at times, loans and grants from bilateral aid donors. It is therefore not surprising that most African governments, even those under intense financial pressure, have tried to continue servicing their debts to the IFIs.

Foreign exchange paid to service debt means less foreign exchange available to finance imports. The impact of debt servicing on foreign-exchange availabilities is typically measured by comparing the amount of debt servicing to the amount of foreign exchange earned from exports in any one year. In 1989, the low-income, debt-distressed African countries paid an equivalent of 24 percent of their export earnings in debt servicing. This is less than the average for Latin America, which was just over 30 percent, or for North Africa and the Middle East, which was just under 30 percent. Although these African countries enjoy lower debt service ratios than a number of better-off developing countries, debt servicing remains a considerable economic burden for many of them.

These statistics provide a snapshot of the current state of indebtedness of the low-income, debt-distressed countries of sub-Saharan Africa, excluding Nigeria. A moving picture of these statistics over the past decade would show several interesting trends. First, the stock of debt has crept upward since 1987 at a rate of about 2 percent per year. This is a markedly slower rate of increase than was the case during the early and mid–1980s, when the stock of debt of these countries rose by nearly 20 percent per year. At that time debt relief consisted in consolidating arrears and payments due, applying a market rate of interest to the consolidated debt, and rescheduling it for repayment in the future. More recently, a proportion of low-income African debt has been canceled and a proportion rescheduled on longer terms at more concessional rates of interest. This has contributed to a slowing of the increase in the stock of debt.

Second, debt servicing, which currently absorbs nearly a quarter of these countries' export earnings, has been trending downward from highs in the mid-1980s of around 30 percent. This improvement is in part due to modest increases in export earnings, combined with a small decline in outlays for debt servicing. In sum, the moving picture of low-income African debt is one in which debt stock and debt-servicing burdens are no longer getting dramatically larger, but neither are they becoming significantly smaller.

NIGERIA

Nigeria, as black Africa's largest economy, a major petroleum producer, and a major debtor to private as well as public creditors, is in a class by itself. Despite its size and petroleum resources, Nigeria is among the world's 20 poorest countries, with a per capita income in 1988 estimated at $290. The economy is heavily dependent on petroleum, with nearly 90 percent of export earnings deriving solely from petroleum sales abroad. Nigerian debt totaled $33 billion in 1989, or nearly 120 percent of the country's GNP. Just under half of this debt was owed to public creditors, mostly foreign governments. Another $16 billion was owed to private creditors. All but $1.2 billion of these credits carried Nigerian government guarantees.

In 1989, Nigeria paid $1.8 billion to service its debt. Just over 50 percent of this servicing was of private credits (including short-term credits). Another $400 million was paid to multilateral development institutions. A final $200 million went to service debts to foreign governments.

In March 1991, Nigeria signed an innovative debt-rescheduling agreement with its private creditors. Creditor banks can choose from a menu of options for the handling of the debt owed to them: they can agree to a buyback of their loans at the market price (roughly 42 cents on the dollar at the time the agreement was signed); they can exchange the debt they hold for registered bonds, at 6.2 percent annual interest, with the principal repayable in the year 2020; or they can exchange the debt for registered bonds paying the London interbank offer rate (LIBOR) plus 13/16 percent, repayable over 20 years with 10 years grace. Under the third option, banks would be required to make new loans equal to 10 percent of the amount rescheduled.

SEVERELY INDEBTED MIDDLE-INCOME AFRICA

Another three African countries particularly heavily burdened with external debt are Senegal, Cote d'Ivoire, and Congo, with per capita incomes in 1988 of $650, $770, and $910, respectively. Like the low-income African countries, their economies are underdeveloped, rely on the production and export of a few primary products, and have suffered low or negative growth in per capita incomes over the past decade. All of these countries are part of the CFA franc zone, with their common currency tied to the French franc at a fixed rate. The CFA franc is widely viewed as overvalued, thus overstating the GNPs of these countries when calculated in dollars.

The stock of debt of these middle-income countries in 1989 totaled $24 billion. Just over a quarter of this total was owed to foreign governments. Another 18 percent was owed to multilateral institutions. Thirty-seven percent was owed to private lenders for medium- and long-term loans, and a final 16 percent was owed on short-term private credits or arrears. The debt–GNP ratios of Cote d'Ivoire and Congo are among the highest in the world: 182 percent and 215 percent, respectively.

A look at debt servicing by Congo, Cote d'Ivoire, and Senegal in 1989 shows the following: roughly two-thirds of actual debt servicing by the first two countries involved the servicing of private long-term credits, both government-guaranteed and nonguaranteed. Most of the remainder was paid to multilateral institutions or to short-term lenders. The servicing of bilateral debts, concessional and nonconcessional, was small, representing 3 percent or less of total debt repayments. Senegal, on the other hand, paid $112 million or 29 percent of its debt servicing to foreign governments and only 21 percent to private long-term creditors. All of these countries paid out a substantial proportion of their export earnings to service their foreign debts, with Cote d'Ivoire's debt service ratio reaching 41 percent. The corresponding ratios for Congo and Senegal were 27 percent and 29 percent, respectively.

Trends in the stock of debt compared to GNP and in the debt service ratio differ among the three middle-income, debt-distressed countries. For Congo, the ratio of debt to GNP has changed little since 1985, but the debt service ratio in 1989, although still high, declined from the peaks of the three previous years. This partly reflects an increase in export earnings and partly a decline in the amount paid to service debts. For Cote d'Ivoire and Senegal, changes in the debt picture have not been so encouraging. The debt–GNP ratio in Cote d'Ivoire rose substantially in 1989 from that of previous years, reaching 182 percent, its highest level ever. The debt service ratio has remained between 40 percent and 50 percent since the early 1980s. In Senegal, both the debt-GNP ratio and the debt service ratio have trended upward from levels prevailing in the mid-1980s.

Sources of African Debt

Africa's debt problems were triggered by the economic turmoil of the 1970s. The surges in petroleum and other primary-product prices in the early part of the decade produced foreign-exchange windfalls for many African governments. They spent those increases in foreign exchange—usually on non-revenue-producing activities—and often borrowed additional monies against expected future export revenues. Multinational banks, eager to recycle petrodollars during this time, proved only too willing to lend. When the prices of their exports fell, as nearly all did by the early 1980s, those African governments still enjoying access to foreign commercial credits borrowed further to offset the decline in their export earnings.

In addition to the volatility and, eventually, the decline in the prices of their primary-product exports, Africans faced rapidly rising prices for their manufactured imports during the latter part of the 1970s as a result of increased inflation in the West. As their terms of trade declined, aid flows and export credits to Africa began to rise. (Export credits from public agencies in developed countries rose sharply between 1975 and 1980 and then contracted with the onset of economic crisis in the African countries; see Demirguc-Kunt and Erzan 1991 for more details.) A significant proportion of this aid was in the form of concessional loans rather than grants, adding further to the mounting stock of African debt. Finally, with the collapse in many of their export markets and the drying up of commercial lending in the early 1980s, African governments turned to the IMF and the World Bank for additional loans, adding yet another layer to their external debts.

The rising amount of credits extended to African governments and private enterprises during the 1970s and early 1980s is only a part of Africa's indebtedness and general economic problems. Other important factors involved the way in which windfall export earnings and foreign loans were used: to finance consumption rather than investment, to finance poorly planned and unproductive investments (such as the infamous Inga-Shaba power generation project in Zaire and the overambitious sugar production and refining project in Cote d'Ivoire, as well as many inappropriate aid projects), or to finance too many non-revenue-generating investments (for example, the dramatic expansion of the Nigerian university system). When the debts came due for repayment, Africans often found that they did not have sufficient revenues to service them either from the investments financed by the loans or from general export revenues. The debt problem in Africa is thus part of the broader problems of poor economic management, poor use of borrowed monies, and a sharp deterioration in the terms of trade.

The Economic and Social Impact of Debt on Low-Income Africa

A heavy burden of debt can affect a country's economic performance and prospects in three principal ways. A very large stock of debt can discourage voluntary capital inflows (private inflows and repatriation of capital from abroad) and encourage capital flight. Foreign and domestic entrepreneurs, for example, may be reluctant to invest in a heavily indebted country for fear of future restrictions on their abilities to finance needed imports or to repatriate profits, or because of other economic uncertainties deriving from the claim on national economic resources represented by a large foreign debt. Those nationals with capital may well try to move that capital abroad, into hard currencies, also in reaction to future economic uncertainties associated with a heavy burden of debt.

Most low-income African countries had only limited access to medium- and long-term foreign bank lending before the onset of the debt crisis in the early 1980s. But even that limited access has dried up as a result of their large debts, and their inability to service those debts has helped discourage further commercial lending. Their large debt overhang may also discourage new private investment—although there are other important causes for the dearth of private investment in these countries. Reliable and comprehensive data do not at present exist on the amount of capital that has been expatriated from the countries of low-income Africa, but it is widely believed that capital flight, particularly from Nigeria, has been substantial. One recent study suggests that net capital outflows from sub-Saharan Africa as a whole, although estimated at only $40 billion between 1976 and 1987, "are comparable to flows from a country such as Argentina, Brazil or Venezuela" (Chang and Cumby 1990, 19).[5] Capital flight from Nigeria is estimated to have totaled $17.5 billion, with $11 billion in outflows between 1985 and 1987 alone.

A word must be added on the impact of African debt on the poor. Poverty and economic decline in developing countries are often blamed on the debt crisis. Many see debt as a symbol and even the primary cause of Africa's current economic problems. Some of the more extreme statements on African debt make it seem that debt is causing the death of Third World babies.

5. Another study on capital flight from Africa by Niels Hermes and Robert Lensink (1990) comes to similar conclusions on the relative magnitudes.

These are misleading and dangerous exaggerations. The burden of servicing foreign debt can exacerbate foreign exchange and government budgetary scarcities and deepen recession. And a deepening recession can in turn depress incomes and worsen the economic conditions of the poor. But it is a mistake to attribute Africa's economic decline and the growing number of Africa's poor largely to foreign debt. And it is particularly dangerous to think that, solely by abolishing the debt, the problems of poverty and economic decline can be eliminated. The problem of economic decline and immiseration in Africa is bigger than the debt problem alone. Reducing the burden of debt is important and timely, but it should be part of a broader assault on these problems by both the Africans themselves and their foreign supporters.

3 External Financing of African Economic Reform: Current Arrangements

The extraordinarily complex and difficult development challenges facing sub-Saharan Africa, and the low-income African countries in particular, argue strongly for a concerted and coherent effort on the part of foreign governments, international agencies, and above all the governments of the African countries themselves to address the development problems of the region. Issues of debt relief should be incorporated into this effort, with a priority placed on promoting development and effective reform rather than maximum feasible servicing of debt, the political and commercial interests of foreign governments, or the political or personal interests of African officials.

In the current international management of debt relief, external financing, and reform in Africa, these issues are handled in a variety of diverse fora and often lack consistency in focus or coordination. Moreover, the problems of focus and coordination promise to become worse with the possibility of further debt relief measures, the appearance of new lending agencies in financing economic reforms, and the increasing diversity of objectives put forth by bilateral aid agencies, with the United States in the lead.

The International Management of African Debt

The current system of managing international debt began to take shape in the mid-1950s, when several Latin American governments found they could not fully service their foreign loans (mainly government-guaranteed suppliers' credits). They were followed in the 1960s by Ghana, Indonesia, Pakistan, and India. The current flood of debt reschedulings began with Zaire in the mid–1970s and accelerated after 1982 when Mexico announced it could not service its debt.

At the outbreak of the debt crisis, international debt management was based on a tripartite arrangement involving private and public creditors, the IFIs (primarily the IMF), and individual debtor countries. Much of this arrangement remains in place today. A government that finds itself unable fully to service its debt seeks a rescheduling of its public bilateral debt through the so-called Paris Club (a grouping of creditor governments drawn primarily from treasuries and ministries of finance and chaired by an official of the French Treasury) and of its private debt through the London Club (an ad hoc group of creditor banks, usually chaired by the bank with the largest exposure in the debtor country). Paris Club negotiations normally precede London Club reschedulings. The framework for rescheduling negotiated under Paris Club auspices is usually applied to London Club reschedulings and to reschedulings of debts owed governments, such as those of Eastern Europe and the Soviet Union, that do not participate in the Paris Club.

Before agreeing to a rescheduling, creditor governments or banks typically require the debtor government to have a stabilization agreement approved by the IMF Executive Board. This is to ensure that the debtor government will implement economic reforms aimed at reducing the deficit in its balance of payments and improving its prospects for full servicing of its debt in the future, including repayment of loans from the IMF. A stabilization program with the IMF is normally accompanied by a loan from the Fund to the debtor government, usually on near-commercial terms, intended to ease the downward pressure on import levels resulting from stabilization measures.

This tripartite system has been based upon four principles:

- Debt rescheduling should be provided only in cases of "imminent default."
- The ability to repay debt and not the maintenance of target rates of growth should take priority in rescheduling decisions. In contrast to several cases in the 1960s (including Pakistan), debt rescheduling has not been considered a vehicle for providing aid.
- Rescheduling may involve a lengthening in maturities but should not include a reduction in the principal or interest on outstanding loans. At the beginning of the 1980s there was a fear on the part of the US government that defaults or reductions in the value of debt by major

debtors could destabilize the money center banks whose debt exposure in Latin America was especially high (this issue is discussed in detail in Eichengreen and Lindert 1989). There was also a belief that, if the value of the debt were reduced, debtor governments would have difficulties gaining access to new borrowing. There was concern about the "moral hazard" of debt relief—the danger that a reduction in the value of the credit would benefit debtors and so possibly encourage poor debt and economic management in the future and discourage efforts on their part to service their debts fully. This principle, as we shall see, has been compromised by recent debt relief initiatives.

- There should be comparable treatment of private and public creditors to ensure that the burden of debt reschedulings is fairly allocated.

Prior to a Paris Club negotiation, creditor governments use data provided by the World Bank and the IMF on the debtor country's estimated balance of payments to do their own financial analysis of the debtor's ability to service future debt. They then use that analysis to develop their positions on the terms of debt reschedulings. The objective of this process within the US government, well described by former US Treasury official Alexis Rieffel (1984, 1985), has been "to identify the largest stream of payments to official creditors consistent with the projections underlying the IMF standby arrangement, without exceeding the parameters of a standard rescheduling" (Rieffel 1984, 96).

The system of debt management has changed since the early 1980s. Creditor governments have acknowledged through their support of the Baker and Brady plans (the latter is described below) that many developing countries' debt problems cannot be treated in isolation from considerations of economic growth, and that the value of debt may have to be reduced to preserve a debtor's ability to grow and repay its remaining debts in the future. Creditor governments have also recognized that low-income debtors face particularly difficult development challenges, for which special debt relief measures may be required, including cancellation or substantial reductions in the amount of debt owed.

Despite these adjustments, much of the basic structure of the system of international debt management set up in the 1960s remains, even for low-income Africa. Debt negotiations continue to take place in the Paris and London clubs, where an IMF–approved stabilization agreement (with its emphasis on closing the balance of payments gap) typically remains a precondition. The financial assumptions and projections in the stabilization agreements are still the basis on which debt-rescheduling negotiations are conducted. The Fund continues to provide much of the information and analysis used in Paris Club negotiations, and government representatives at these meetings continue to be drawn primarily from ministries of finance or of economics. The case of the United States is an odd one: US delegations to Paris Club reschedulings have usually been led by officials from the Department of State and included representatives from the Department of the Treasury (who prepare initial financial analyses and drafts of the position papers), the Export-Import Bank, and the Department of Agriculture (to cover loans for food aid and food exports). The US federal agency principally responsible for development affairs, the Agency for International Development (AID), has no involvement in these negotiations or in their preparation. US officials participating in debt reschedulings confirm that their primary focus remains negotiating schedules for the repayment of debt, not providing debtors with assistance to promote their development.

Financing Economic Reform and Development in Africa

In addition to the arrangements for managing debt and stabilization in Africa and elsewhere, another set of international arrangements has grown up for coordinating development financing. For Africa, the principal ones are Consultative Groups (CGs), Roundtables, and the World Bank–chaired Special Program of Assistance (SPA) for low-income, debt-distressed Africa. CGs are World Bank–chaired groups comprising aid-giving governments and a single African government. Roundtables are chaired by the UN Development Program but are otherwise similar to CGs.

CGs meet periodically, usually after the African government has adopted a structural adjustment program, to review the adjustment program and the external financing needs of the African government.

The Bank provides participants with estimates of future financing needs; these estimates are typically based on target rates of growth, the quantity of imports necessary to achieve those targets, expected export earnings, debt relief, aid, other capital inflows and outflows, and the uncovered financing gap. Representatives of donor governments attending a CG meeting normally review their plans for future aid for the participating African government, but these meetings are not negotiating or pledging sessions. They are more in the nature of sensitivity-raising exercises for developed-country governments through which the Bank attempts to encourage those governments to provide needed resources to the participating African country. CGs are also used as an incentive and reward for African governments undertaking acceptable reform programs and a concrete demonstration that the Bank approves of those reforms.

The SPA, created by the World Bank in 1987, is a vehicle through which the World Bank attempts to mobilize concessional assistance and debt relief adequate to finance reform programs in low-income, debt-distressed African countries. The SPA includes member governments of the World Bank and international institutions providing aid to Africa. It meets semiannually to discuss overall reform efforts in Africa, the policies and programs of developed countries and international institutions relating to African reform and development, and the external financing needs of African governments. Every three years, on the basis of Bank estimates of African external financing needs for the coming three-year period (based on an aggregated gap analysis similar to that done for individual African countries), donor governments and institutions discuss the course of reform in eligible African countries and pledge external financing for reforms for the coming triennium. The SPA is an organization of aid donors and creditors; it does not include African governments as members. It has become a venue for discussions by aid donors on their development policies toward severely indebted low-income African countries in adjustment. The SPA does not coordinate or negotiate external financing on a country-specific level.[1]

---

1. For more detail on the SPA, see World Bank (1990c).

Finally, there are at times ad hoc arrangements for coordinating aid loans and grants in individual African capitals. This is at once one of the most important and one of the weakest elements in the international dimension of reform and development in Africa. What foreign governments actually finance in African countries can at times diverge dramatically from what the overall policy statements of their governments call for, can differ as well from the policy priorities of the African governments, and can even conflict with the development programs of other aid-giving governments or international institutions. There is no systematic approach to coordinating external financing in African capitals. Whether coordination groups exist, who chairs them, what donors and sectors they include, whether they include African officials or not, how long they last, and what influence they have all vary enormously, depending on the country and the personal inclinations and abilities of African economic officials and their foreign counterparts.

In sum, two clusters of international arrangements have evolved over the past decade and a half for managing the external dimension of African reform and development. One cluster is focused on stabilization and debt management and is led by the IMF; the other is focused on economic growth and is usually led by the World Bank. Arrangements in African capitals remain ad hoc. There is obvious potential for incoherence and conflict between the goals and advice to Africans on reform and development programs. Not surprisingly, conflicts have occurred: for example, Africans have been advised by the Fund to avoid decreases in tariffs in order to maintain or increase public revenues, at the same time as they were being pressed by the Bank to liberalize trade and lower tariffs in order to promote domestic competition.

A more subtle problem can occur when an African government, like that of Kenya, undertakes an effective stabilization program and gains the approval and support of the IMF but resists implementing needed structural adjustment programs supported by the World Bank. (The opposite situation has at times prevailed in Tanzania, where the government has resisted stabilization but implemented adjustment programs.) A government in that position can use the approval of one of the Bretton Woods institutions to counter the pressures for reform from the other or from developed-country governments. A more pernicious problem can involve aid or mixed credits provided by foreign governments pursuing primarily commercial objectives for projects (often overpriced) of low priority in African countries, thus undermining reform and development strategies and adding to debt. Cases of conflict or incoherence among the large number of foreign-government agencies or international institutions supporting African reform are rarely documented, but anecdotal evidence suggests that they are far from rare.

The Bretton Woods institutions have recognized the potential for conflict and have made an effort over the past half-decade to coordinate their policies regarding reform in Africa and elsewhere. A major vehicle for that coordination is the Policy Framework Paper (PFP). The PFP sets out a comprehensive program of economic reforms to take place over a three-year period, including both medium-term policy objectives and external financing needs. The existence of a PFP is a requirement for any government borrowing from the IMF under the Structural Adjustment Facility (SAF) or the Enhanced Structural Adjustment Facility (ESAF), which are described below. As a framework encompassing reform policies to be pursued by a developing country, usually over a period of three years, the PFP was intended to ensure coherence between Bank and Fund policies in individual countries. Other arrangements, including periodic consultations between Bank and Fund staff working on particular countries and joint missions, also exist to promote Bank-Fund collaboration.

There are no published evaluations of whether the PFPs and other efforts at coordination between the Bretton Woods institutions have in fact promoted greater coherence in their reform programs or have reduced conflicts among the myriad aid-giving agencies involved in Africa. Both the World Bank and the IMF continue to produce their own program documents, which, however, are theoretically based on the PFP. Many African officials as well as Bank and Fund staff acknowledge privately that it is Fund staff, not the relevant African officials, who typically produce the first draft of the PFP. This provides the Fund with an added measure of influence over the final product and potentially over the shape of the overall reform program. However, it is not clear how much of a relationship the PFPs have to African reform programs in practice or what the IFIs and foreign governments actually finance with their aid. The PFP documents themselves are so broad and contain so many planned reforms, typically stated in very general terms and often without priorities or timetables, that their usefulness as road maps of economic reform or as instruments for avoiding policy conflicts among the Bank, the Fund, and other agencies is questionable.

In any case, the problems of policy coherence between the Fund and the Bank in African countries and between the clusters of international arrangements aimed at managing debt and stabilization and promoting development go beyond the potential for conflict within individual reform programs. Because negotiations on Fund-sponsored stabilization programs are typically a precondition both for debt reschedulings and for negotiations on World Bank structural adjustment loans,[2] Fund programs and Fund estimates of financing gaps can influence the emphasis and timing of particular economic reforms as well as the analysis of financing gaps utilized in international discussions of African economic reform and financing programs.

The priority placed on balance of payments stabilization, debt servicing, and closing of a balance of payments financing gap (rather than an import financing gap associated with target rates of growth) is often echoed in developed-country governments where ministries of finance rather than development agencies typically take the lead in shaping their governments' positions on stabilization and debt-rescheduling agreements, which often precede or are taken independently of government positions on structural adjustment programs and development financing. Coordination on these issues within creditor governments and between aid agencies and ministries of finance varies, but if US practice is anything to go by, it remains limited at best: there the Treasury and the Department of State retain control over questions of the repayment of debts to the US government, with little input from AID, and conversely AID handles development issues with little input from the Treasury and episodic input from the Department of State.

2. An IMF stabilization program is not normally a precondition for a World Bank-financed sector adjustment loan (SECAL), although a stabilization program has typically been a precondition for the structural adjustment loans (SALs). SECALs are narrower in focus than SALs and smaller in the amount of their credits. They have become increasingly numerous in recent years in Bank lending operations in Africa.

It seems very likely that the problems of policy coherence and coordination among international and bilateral aid donors to Africa may worsen in coming years with changes, already apparent, in aid programs for the region. One important change is the entry by the European Development Fund (EDF) into substantial lending for structural adjustment. The EDF is at present the largest single source of concessional aid to the countries of sub-Saharan Africa, committing $2.9 billion to the region in 1988 (Development Assistance Committee 1990, 229). Most of its aid in the past has financed discrete projects. However, the EDF has recently decided to allocate a substantial proportion of its lending in Africa to support structural adjustment and is now beginning to hire staff to manage those lending operations. It is as yet unclear whether the EDF will be content to follow the lead of the IMF and the World Bank in the reform programs it finances in Africa, whether it will attempt to differentiate its approach to stabilization and adjustment from those of the Bretton Woods institutions, or whether it will claim a leadership role in the shaping and financing of reform programs in particular African countries. Issues of coherence and external leadership in development financing have on occasion created tensions between the World Bank and the African Development Bank. There is clearly a possibility of conflict between the World Bank and the EDF on adjustment lending in Africa in the future.

A second and perhaps more troubling problem of coherence in the reform policies urged on African governments involves bilateral aid donors, in particular the United States. With the decline in US–Soviet Cold War competition in Africa and elsewhere, a major pillar of the US foreign aid program—that of protecting US security and political interests abroad through containing efforts by the Soviets to spread their influence—has crumbled. The search is clearly on in Washington for rationales to replace the long-held security rationale. One approach favored by some in Congress and in the administration is to justify US aid by linking it to the spread of US "core values" abroad, specifically democracy. This is, in effect, an extension of the human rights policy initiated by the Carter administration to include political rights associated with democracy. A recent document published by AID states that "Within each region of the world, allocations of A.I.D. funds to individual countries will take into account their progress toward democratization. This will place democracy on a comparable footing with progress in economic reforms and the establishment of a market-oriented economy... ." (AID 1990, 3).

Another rationale, this one emerging from the US Senate, is already finding resonance in US aid programs. This approach would link an annually increasing proportion of US aid to the promotion of US exports abroad, particularly construction projects. It is reflected in a bill introduced in the 100th and 101st Congresses by Senators Robert C. Byrd (D-WV), Lloyd Bentsen (D-TX), Max S. Baucus (D-MT), and David L. Boren (D-OK). It would be hard to find a more influential group of senators: Senator Byrd chairs the Senate Appropriations Committee and Senator Bentsen the Finance Committee. The White House reportedly opposes the bill, but whether Congress passes it or not, these senators' views will be taken very seriously in the administration. Indeed, AID is already responding to their initiative by allocating an increasing proportion of its aid to Asian countries for promoting US exports.

All of this groping for a reason to continue US aid abroad produces an extraordinary degree of uncertainty about how US aid will be used in the future and which foreign governments will receive it. It is possible that if the United States decides to concentrate its aid in countries that are already democratic or are in the process of democratizing, or if it conditions its aid on progress toward democracy, those governments that are implementing serious adjustment programs but that are not democratic—for example, Ghana—will find their external support reduced. Some countries may also face a trade-off between continuing stringent adjustment programs and democratizing. If autocratic governments in adjustment decide to democratize, public discontent with reform programs, expressed in political debates and elections, could derail economic reforms. Economic reform and political liberalization are both worthy and needed in much of Africa. But it may not always be possible to implement both together.

Similarly, a US aid program that concentrates on using concessional resources to promote US business abroad could conflict with the goals of structural adjustment. Such an approach could result in a shift of US aid away from the poor countries of Africa, where opportunities for US investors are fewer, to better-off countries in Asia and Latin America.

Or it could be used to encourage African governments to undertake aid-financed projects of low priority or in conflict with their adjustment programs.

If the United States should decide to pursue one or another (or all) of these goals with its aid, a number of other aid-giving governments are likely to follow. The British, Japanese, and other governments are already echoing the emphasis on democratization as a criterion for aid. Similarly, the Italians, the French, and the Japanese have long experience in using their aid to promote their exports. Efforts, long supported by the United States, to limit concessional assistance for export financing or reduce aid tied exclusively to purchases in donor countries will be undermined if the United States becomes an advocate of aid for exports rather than for development or adjustment. Arguments for improved coordination among aid donors on issues of debt, resources, and reform in Africa have rarely been stronger to ensure not only the adequacy and coherence of aid programs but also the sustained support and commitment on the part of aid-giving governments to reforms in the future.

Initiatives on African Debt

The international community has for some time recognized the need to adopt special measures for handling African debt problems. The past several years have witnessed a number of changes in the way that debt is handled, including an expansion in the coverage of Paris Club reschedulings to include previously rescheduled debts, 100 percent of the principal and interest owed during the consolidation period, and rescheduling of arrears. In addition, for low-income countries there has been an increased degree of concessionality in debt reschedulings within the Paris Club, including the cancellation of a proportion of their debt, below-market rates on moratorium interest, and a lengthening of grace and repayment periods. Creditors and debtors have also participated in programs of debt reduction, debt cancellation, debt-for-equity swaps, debt-for-development or -environment swaps, and concessional refinancing of external debt.

The most prominent debt reduction initiative for low-income African countries was the agreement by major creditor governments at the economic summit in Toronto in 1988 to restructure nonconcessional public debt (mainly export credits) within the Paris Club in one of three arrangements. Creditors could choose to cancel one-third of the principal due them during the consolidation period and reschedule the remainder at market rates of interest, to be repaid with an 8-year grace period and 14-year maturities. Or they could choose to reschedule the entire principal but charge below-market rates of interest, again to be repaid over an 8-year grace period and 14-year maturity. A third option was to reschedule all of the debt at market interest rates but with a 14-year grace period and a 25-year maturity period.

The agreement on the Toronto menu approach broke with past creditor-government practice in resisting any rescheduling of nonconcessional bilateral public debts on concessional terms. The United States agreed for the first time that concessional interest rates could be applied by other creditors in such reschedulings, although it refused to provide concessional interest rates itself. As of September 1990, 17 low-income African countries had rescheduled $5 billion of their debt under Toronto terms. Several countries had done so more than once. (These terms have recently been extended to Senegal, which is classified as middle-income but is poor enough to be eligible to borrow from the International Development Association [IDA], the World Bank's soft loan window.) Rescheduling under the Toronto approach is estimated to have provided low-income African countries a cash flow savings, compared with what would have been the case under a standard rescheduling, of $100 million over an average consolidation period of 17 months. This savings remains a small proportion—roughly 2 percent—of the debt servicing due during that period. That proportion is expected to increase in the future but still to have only a modest impact on debt servicing.[3]

3. See World Bank (1990a, vol. I and Summary Tables, 47) on the implementation and impact of the Toronto menu approach.

Since 1987, Belgium, France, Germany, the United Kingdom, the United States, and other creditor governments have announced their willingness to cancel nearly $1.6 billion owed them by low-income African governments, largely in concessional loans. The $1.6 billion in canceled debt was equal to roughly 2 percent of the total stock of low-income African debt in 1987. The cancellations will likely have a minor impact on actual debt servicing, since much of the canceled debt would likely have been rescheduled. One aspect of debt cancellation initiatives worth noting here is that, while creditor governments have emphasized that they cancel debt on a case-by-case basis according to whether debtors need the relief or are implementing economic reforms, this is not always the case. For example, the country most vociferous in its commitment to a case-by-case approach, the United States, canceled $745 million in African debt in 1990–91, including nearly $200 million in Zairian debt and $175 million in Kenyan debt.[4] Neither Kenya nor Zaire can be considered a good performer in the area of economic reform. Both have poor human rights records. Kenya has never sought a Paris Club debt rescheduling and has paid its debts to the US government regularly. It appears that the debt of these two countries was canceled because they are classified as low-income African countries, and the administration wished to avoid the political problems with their governments that might have resulted from denying them debt relief while other low-income African countries were receiving such relief. Cancellation of the debt of these countries raises questions about the US commitment to a case-by-case approach to debt relief, sends their governments (and others) the wrong signals about the importance of economic reform, and discredits administration promises of providing debt relief only to the deserving.

The World Bank and the IMF have also implemented programs aimed at easing the immediate burden on low-income countries of servicing earlier loans, now maturing, from these institutions. In 1988, the World Bank set aside 10 percent of IDA reflows and investment income to ease the interest payments on World Bank loans for qualifying low-

4. For details, see AID (1991, 44–46).

income countries. (Some of these countries, like Zambia, had at one time had per capita income levels high enough to be eligible to borrow from the World Bank on its harder terms. They still had to service those loans, although the countries had since been reclassified as low-income and debt-distressed.) The Bank has supplemented these funds with others to provide nine low-income, debt-distressed countries with concessional loans sufficient to finance 60 percent of their interest payments to the World Bank. Bank staff have imaginatively labeled this program "the fifth dimension."

In addition, in September 1989, the Bank announced the establishment of a $100 million Debt Reduction Facility for low-income countries. This facility, financed from the Bank's net income, will make up to $10 million in grants to individual debtors to buy back private debt at deep discounts (expected to exceed 80 percent in some cases).[5] One of the first African governments to take advantage of this arrangement was Niger, which in February 1991 reached agreement with its private creditors to buy back its entire $108 million in private debt at 18 cents on the dollar. of its face value. Under this agreement, banks can choose between receiving 18 percent of their outstanding loans immediately or receiving repayment at 100 percent of the face value in 21 years. Repayment is to be guaranteed through the purchase by Niger of zero-coupon US government bonds. At the time of this writing, Mozambique was negotiating similar arrangements, and another 13 governments have applied for funds from the World Bank's debt reduction facility.

In recent years the largest net negative resource flows from low-income Africa to any creditor institution have been to the IMF; these flows have exceeded $200 million per year since 1986. In that same year, the IMF set up its Structural Adjustment Facility (SAF), and in 1987 it established an Enhanced Structural Adjustment Facility (ESAF) to make loans on concessional terms to low-income countries with chronic balance of payments problems. Together, the SAF and the

---

5. A recent report on international loan trading by Salomon Brothers ("Memorandum to Portfolio Managers," 29 April 1991) shows indicative cash prices for Cote d'Ivoire debt at 6 cents on the dollar, for Zaire at 16 cents on the dollar, and for Nigeria at 42 cents on the dollar. There is not much trading activity on most of this debt.

ESAF can lend $12 billion to low-income countries with chronic balance of payments problems. The terms of SAF and ESAF loans are 10 years repayment, 5 years grace, with an interest rate of 0.5 percent. By March 1991, SAF and ESAF loans of $1.9 billion had been committed to 16 low-income African countries, with $1.2 billion actually disbursed (*IMF Survey* 1 April, 1991, 99). By April 1991, $2.0 billion had been obligated to 20 African countries, with $1.1 billion disbursed. (It was originally intended that all of the ESAF monies would be obligated by the end of 1989. The slowness of ESAF commitments was a result of the tough conditionality required by the Fund for ESAF loans.)

The SAF and ESAF arrangements must be seen as a temporary palliative to ease the burden on low-income African governments of servicing their debts to the Fund. It is now clear that the relatively hard terms of normal IMF lending (three- to five-year credits at near market rates of interest) are inappropriate for most low-income African borrowers, whose economic problems have proven to be far more deep seated and difficult to resolve than was assumed in the early 1980s when many of these countries first approached the Fund for loans. The SAF and ESAF arrangements help in easing the current burden of servicing debts to the Fund by making new loans on far softer terms—in effect refinancing a proportion of existing debt repurchase (i.e., repayment) obligations. SAF and ESAF loans also permit the Fund to establish stabilization programs for the first time with some of the world's poorest countries, such as Chad and Mozambique, which could not reasonably be expected to borrow on standard IMF terms. But even the SAF and ESAF arrangement is a temporary and partial solution to the problem of refinancing IMF loans or financing new lending on terms appropriate to African needs. It is likely that in the 1990s, as SAF and ESAF loans mature, the international community will again face the need to help refinance debts of low-income African countries to the Fund.

More exotic debt reduction measures have also been tried in low-income Africa. Nigeria is believed to have swapped as much as $2 billion in debt for equity in 1989. Several other African countries have reportedly swapped smaller amounts. However, there are limits on how much debt Africans can expect to swap for equity, given the poor state of their economies and investors' reluctance to risk their funds in the region.

Other exotic debt reduction schemes have involved debt-for-nature swaps, debt-for-development swaps, and debt buybacks. The few cases in which these approaches were used include an AID–financed $1 million debt-for-nature swap in Madagascar and a Marine Midland Bank conversion of $800,000 of its Sudanese debt to local currency for use by nongovernmental organizations.

In 1989, the United States announced its support of voluntary reductions in private debt in a scheme now termed the Brady Plan. In effect, commercial banks would reduce the value of the debt owed them by individual debtors and/or provide new lending to those debtors in exchange for stronger guarantees of future repayments of interest and principal. In the case of Mexico, the guarantee of principal was provided through conversions of debt obligations into bonds backed by zero-coupon US Treasury bonds. Interest payments would be backed in part with IMF guarantees. Apparently after considerable pressure from the Treasury, US banks agreed to voluntary debt reduction arrangements for Mexico, the Philippines, Costa Rica, Morocco, Venezuela, and Uruguay. Other potential participants in a Brady Plan include Congo and Cote d'Ivoire, but no negotiations appear to be in the offing for these countries.

Finally, there is the problem of massive arrears to the IMF accumulated by a number of low-income African countries. Sudan, Zambia, Sierra Leone, Liberia, and Somalia are currently in arrears to the Fund, the first two countries owing over $1 billion each. Countries in arrears must clear those arrears before a new IMF stabilization program can be activated. Some member states have viewed the arrears as also threatening the financial health of the Fund itself. In the past, when a government in arrears was ready to sign a new stabilization agreement with the Fund, foreign governments or commercial banks would make "bridge loans" (short-term credits to pay off the arrears), and those bridge loans would be repaid with new credits from the Fund. This approach may still be feasible with smaller debtors like Somalia or Liberia, but it will not work with Sudan and Zambia where arrears have become prohibitively large. Sudan does not at present appear ready to negotiate and implement a stabilization program with the IMF. And even the smaller debtors, once they emerge from their internal conflict and the breakdown of their governments, may be so devastated and impoverished that they will simply be unable to service any debts for the foreseeable future. This trio of unfortunate countries, plus others (possibly Ethiopia) that may suffer from similar conflicts and breakdowns in political order in the future, will, once responsible governments are reestablished, present the international community with particularly difficult debt and development challenges if they are not to be entirely shut out of the existing international financial system.

Efforts are now under way to deal with the large Zambian debt to the IFIs. This approach requires the Zambian government to implement a "shadow" IMF program (stabilization measures acceptable to the Fund but without Fund lending) for two to three years and to remain current in servicing its loans from the Fund. During the period of the shadow program, the Zambians acquire a claim to borrow from the ESAF in the future in amounts sufficient to clear past arrears. IMF gold would be used as collateral against future repayments of ESAF loans to Zambia. Thus far, the arrangement for clearing Zambian arrears has progressed well. Recently, Zambia paid off its arrears to the World Bank through a combination of increased aid from developed-country governments and a bridge loan from the Bank of England. New lending from the World Bank then permitted Zambia to repay its bridge loan to the British bank. Now that its arrears to the World Bank have been eliminated, Zambia can again borrow—but at the cost of an increase in its stock of debt and future debt servicing. It is not clear that a Zambia-style arrangement will be sensible or feasible for poorer, war-torn African countries in arrears to the IFIs.

Other initiatives involving Africa debt have been proposed. The African Development Bank has developed a "securitization" proposal in which public and private debt (except that owed to multilateral creditors) would be consolidated into 20-year notes with rates of interest set according to what debtors could reasonably be expected to pay (most likely below-market rates). Debtors would make annual payments into a redemption fund, which would be managed by a board of trustees to ensure that the notes would be paid off at maturity. This proposal has been the subject of considerable discussion, but the complex negotiations it implies and its probably unrealistic presumption that debtors could pay enough into a redemption fund over 20 years to retire the notes have limited the enthusiasm of key creditors for this idea. It appears unlikely ever to be implemented.

In 1987, a special meeting of the Organization of African Unity, convened to consider Africa's debt crisis, called for a 10-year moratorium on African debt repayments. In 1988, a UN report, *Financing Africa's Recovery,* recommended that creditors cancel all concessional debt owed them by debt-distressed African countries and that nonconcessional credits due over the coming three years be consolidated and rescheduled on IDA terms, in effect providing a three-year moratorium on debt servicing. Other groups of debtor countries have called for cancellation of their debts. In 1990, creditor governments promised to cancel roughly $4 billion of the debt of severely indebted low-income African countries (out of a total debt stock in 1989 of $102 billion, including $45 billion of bilateral debt). No action has been taken on other elements in these proposals.

Several other initiatives have recently been proposed to alleviate the debt burdens of low-income countries. The proposal that has received the most attention was made in September 1990 by John Major, at that time Chancellor of the Exchequer in the UK government. At a meeting of the finance ministers of the Commonwealth in Trinidad, Major proposed four modifications in the Toronto terms for debt restructuring. Under Major's plan:

- The terms would cover the entire stock of debt rather than only the debt due during a one- to two-year consolidation period;
- The write-off of debt would be expanded from one-third to two-thirds of the total;
- Interest payments due during the first five years after the debt is restructured, together with the principal due, should be repaid in gradually increasing amounts, based on the growth in export capacity of the debtor country's economy;
- The maturities of the restructured debts should be extended from 14 to 24 years.

This proposal quickly became known as the "Trinidad terms." It was considerably more concessional that the Toronto terms and would restructure an individual country's public debt all at once rather than in successive consolidation periods. It seems likely that the Trinidad terms will be discussed at the 1991 economic summit in London in July 1991.

A second proposal on debt relief for low-income countries was made in 1990 by Jan Pronk, the Minister for Development Cooperation of the Netherlands. He proposed simply that creditor governments cancel all the debt owed them by the least-developed debt-distressed countries, in return for a commitment by these countries to implement sound economic policies.

A 1990 UN report entitled *Africa's Commodity Problems: Toward a Solution* (also known as the Fraser report after Malcolm Fraser, the chairman of its study group) recommended a 3- to 10-year moratorium on all bilateral public debt servicing by African countries, combined with rescheduling on highly concessional terms.

World Bank officials and others have continued to raise the problem of the severely indebted middle-income African countries, particularly Cote d'Ivoire and Congo. These countries have thus far benefited only minimally from debt reduction initiatives. Because they are classified as middle-income, they have not been offered Toronto terms in their debt reschedulings. Yet because they are among the poorest of the middle-income category (which includes countries with annual per capita incomes of from $500 to $6,000), they have less access to concessional aid than the poorer countries. Because of their heavy debt burdens and comparatively low level of development, they have little access to new commercial lending. And because their total commercial debt is small in global terms and their immediate economic prospects are poor, they have not benefited from reschedulings under the Brady Plan.

Although Nigeria is now classified as a low-income country, it faces many of the same problems as the middle-income debt-distressed countries. In its most recent rescheduling negotiations with the Paris Club, Nigeria sought but was been denied Toronto terms, in part as a result of the increase in its export earnings arising from the (temporary) surge in petroleum prices at the beginning of the Persian Gulf crisis. Nigeria's size and petroleum reserves have also dampened its access to bilateral concessional aid.

Finally, there has been a recent spate of debt reduction initiatives coming out of Washington for countries of political importance to the United States. These include the Enterprise for the Americas and the

Egyptian and Polish debt reduction initiatives. Each of these is different from the others, and each suggests ways in which the US or other governments might provide further debt relief to low- and middle-income, debt-distressed African countries.

THE ENTERPRISE FOR THE AMERICAS

On 20 June 1990, President George Bush announced a three-part plan for helping Latin American countries confront their economic problems. The debt reduction part of the Enterprise plan would reduce the principal and restructure concessional interest rates on $7 billion in concessional economic credits (aid and PL480), accept interest payments in local currency to be allocated to environmental projects, and sell a proportion of outstanding commercial credits (of the Export-Import Bank and the Commodity Credit Corporation [CCC]) at below face value, possibly to the debtor government for payment in local currencies, and use the proceeds for debt-equity or debt-for-nature swaps. To qualify for these debt reduction schemes, Latin American governments would have to have economic reform programs in place. The administration will have to obtain legislative authorization on the arrangements involving Eximbank, the CCC, and aid debt reduction proposals.[6]

DEBT RELIEF FOR EGYPT

In September 1990, President Bush asked Congress to authorize the cancellation of $6.7 billion in military debt owed by the government of Egypt to the US government. This initiative was in effect a reward for Egypt's support for US policy in the Gulf crisis. The most interesting aspect of the debt reduction scheme for Egypt is the imaginative way in which its budgetary impact was handled. The administration argued

6. For more details on the Enterprise for the Americas see Serafino and Cody (1991).

that the cancellation of Egypt's military debt would have no impact on the US budget since Egypt's servicing of this debt was projected by the Office of Management and Budget (OMB) at zero. This was a controversial assumption to some in Congress, since the Egyptians had been making payments on this debt. In fact, in 1989 they had repaid over $500 million in military debt to the US government. The final figures on the budgetary impact were negotiated between the Congress and the adminstration, and set at not more than $207 million in 1991 and a total of $1.8 billion over five years. These figures are presumed to include the impact of Polish debt reduction as well (Nowels 1991, 9).

Another noteworthy aspect of the Egyptian debt reduction scheme was the effort by the United States to persuade other creditor governments to reduce Egypt's debt to them. These governments proved less forthcoming than the United States, however, arguing that Egypt lacks a stabilization agreement with the IMF and should not benefit from debt relief until an IMF–approved stabilization program is in place. Secretary of State James A. Baker III is reported to have promised to help the Egyptians in their negotiations with the Fund. There is a clear danger here of a powerful member of the Fund, wanting an IMF agreement for primarily political reasons, exerting its influence on the Fund to facilitate agreements with favored foreign governments. This is not a new phenomenon, but if it should become more common it could politicize the Fund and undermine the credibility of the institution.

THE POLISH DEBT INITIATIVE

The Bush administration's initiative on Polish debt reduction was a result of congressional pressures to help Poland as it implements dramatic economic and political reforms. In section 562 of the 1991 foreign aid appropriations act of 1989 (passed in late 1990), the Congress prohibited any US contributions to the European Bank for Reconstruction and Development until the administration provided debt relief to Poland.

The bilateral public debt of the Polish government to the US government amounts to $3.8 billion, just over 10 percent of Poland's total foreign debt. In 1991, the United States agreed to cancel 70 percent of that debt in a complicated rescheduling arrangement under Paris Club auspices. The Bush administration was unsuccessful in persuading Poland's other creditor governments to provide such generous relief, although others did reduce the value of their outstanding credits by half. Polish debt relief involves both the cancellation and concessional rescheduling of debts owed to the Eximbank and the CCC. This marks the first time that Eximbank loans have been canceled. (The Congress has already provided the administration with the authority to do so for Poland.)

The latter half of 1990 and the first half of 1991 have seen a rapid evolution in US policies on bilateral debt relief—but only for governments that are politically important to the United States. This selectivity has been noted—and criticized—by other creditor countries, including Germany and Japan. These initiatives set interesting precedents for the treatment of debt for Africa and other poor countries, but they also impart a degree of chaos to the management of international debt, and they point to an urgent need for a system in which economic need and performance rather than political favoritism play the principal roles in how foreign debt and external financing in general is managed.

4 A New Program for Financing Reform in Low-Income Africa

The urgency of the development problems facing most of Africa, and especially the severely indebted countries of low-income Africa, argues for a more coherent and more focused approach to the external dimnesion of reform and development for these countries. This approach should include a new initiative on debt. But in order not to undermine the incentives for reform, any new initiative on debt should link debt reduction and debt relief to development needs and to performance on economic reform. This study presents one such initiative. The proposal involves the merging of CGs, Roundtables, and other coordinating groups plus the Paris Club meetings into a single international grouping for individual countries—called here an Adjustment Review Consortium (ARC)—to be chaired by the World Bank with participation by creditor and donor governments and international institutions plus the individual African government.[1]

The Design of an ARC

The ARC would amalgamate and extend the functions of the Paris Club and the World Bank–chaired consultative groups (and the Roundtables chaired by the UN Development Program). Its scope of responsibility would encompass economic reform and development as well as external financing issues involving the participating African government, including the quantity, terms, and use of concessional aid and debt relief and

1. An alternative would be to have the ARC chaired by an experienced individual not currently associated with either of the Bretton Woods institutions—for example, by former presidents or senior officials of IFIs.

reduction. Participation by an African government in an ARC would be voluntary. Before an ARC would be set up, the African government would have adopted stabilization and/or structural adjustment programs acceptable to the World Bank. The ARC would meet periodically (for example, every two years) to review the African participant's progress in implementing its economic reform and development programs, to assess the African participant's plans for such programs over the coming two-year period, and to review, negotiate, and coordinate the amount and use of debt relief and aid flows required to support future reform and development programs. The assistance programs of individual aid donors would also be subject to review by all participants and, where appropriate, criticism and recommendations for change.

Where the African government's past progress on reform has been satisfactory and plans for future reform are adequate, creditor governments would be expected to cancel or reschedule on highly concessional terms the debt owed them for the coming performance period, thus reducing both the amount of debt servicing and the stock of debt in present-value terms. In addition, developed-country governments and the IFIs would commit appropriate amounts of aid to support target import and investment levels based on economically desirable and politically feasible growth rates. The World Bank, with assistance from the IMF, would provide the backup information and analysis on the debtor's past adjustment performance, future adjustment plans, and financing needs. A Policy Framework Paper outlining a realistic medium-term reform program, including macro- and microeconomic reforms and investment plans, and priorities and approximate schedules for implementing reforms as well as long term growth strategies, could provide the basis for this review. The first draft of the PFP should be prepared by the African government, with assistance where needed from the World Bank and the IMF.

Should the participating African government fail to make satisfactory progress toward reform, creditors and aid donors might decide to terminate, delay, or scale down the amount of their relief or assistance, renegotiate the ARC agreement, or withdraw from or cancel the ARC altogether. The African government could choose to terminate its participation in the ARC at any time. In the case of cancellation of the ARC, the handling of aid and debt issues would revert to existing mechanisms.

Debt relief and aid commitments would be conditioned on economic reforms and would extend to issues of governance, but participants would focus primarily on governance as it affects economic performance. Operationally, it may be difficult to delineate a firm boundary between those governance issues that mainly affect economic performance and more general problems of the behavior of governments as it affects human, civil, and political rights. Multilateral agencies and foreign governments participating in an ARC would have to exercise good judgment in addressing these issues, bearing in mind the urgency of effective economic reform and development and their own limited capacity to prescribe workable and sustainable political reforms for other societies. Conditions of good economic governance would typically include transparent budgeting (in central and local government agencies as well as state-owned enterprises), open and competitive bidding on large public investment projects, consistency between major public expenditure decisions and plans and commitments in the PFP,[2] and fair, timely, and consistent implementation of laws and regulations affecting trade, investment, and other economic activities.

Some of these elements of good economic governance could be made preconditions for an ARC. Others—for example, the consistent implementation of laws and regulations (particularly important for private investors)—may be more difficult to monitor and assess, since many decisions on these issues are made by various government agencies, administrative and judicial, over a given period of time. There may be a number of feasible approaches to dealing with this difficult type of governance problem. One such approach might include establishment, in the individual African country, of an Investment Center (IC), to be governed by a board of directors drawn from the foreign and domestic public and private sectors (and possibly including some officials of foreign governments), to act as a source of information on investment opportunities and on laws and regulations governing that investment, as a provider of licenses and possibly of credit, and as an ombudsman

2. The World Bank has a lending instrument—the Public Expenditure Review Loans (PERLs)—aimed at review and surveillance of all public expenditure programs. The approach now used in PERLs could be extended to all African ARC participants, although the public expenditure review would not necessarily have a loan attached to it.

for domestic and foreign investors. Establishment of an IC should be accompanied by a streamlining and possibly consolidation or reduction of the laws and regulations governing investment in a manner consistent with national interests, in order to speed decisions and reduce opportunities for local bureaucrats to delay decisions or extract rents (in the form of kickbacks, side payments, or "commissions") for approving them.

The degree of the IC's authority in all of these areas could be decided by the Africans and foreign governments and could be linked to the amount of financial support (for overhead and credit programs) the latter would be willing to provide such centers. Ideally, the IC would function to enhance the accountability and predictability of African governments in their dealings with private investors. Should these governments behave in unfair ways toward private investors, foreign governments could reduce or terminate their support and participation in an IC or even in an ARC itself.

The inclusion of considerations of economic governance in an ARC raises several issues. First, it might be argued that there is no need to include such considerations in reform programs, because they are already included in PFPs. This may well be so, but in too many cases PFPs are still not taken seriously either by the aid donors or by the African recipients. Were it otherwise, problems of governance would not continue to be so prominent, and a number of African governments now receiving World Bank adjustment loans or IMF ESAF loans would likely be fewer.

Another objection to this approach might be that the conditions associated with loans for stabilization or restructuring are already too numerous, too burdensome, and too intrusive. The current PFP for Zambia, which contains nearly 140 reform strategies and measures in nearly every sector to be implemented between 1989 and 1993, appears to confirm that criticism. World Bank and AID staff have worried in private that where there are so many conditions associated with adjustment lending, lenders cannot (and do not) enforce all of those conditions, or do not suspend lending operations when the African government fails to fulfill particular conditions. Programs of conditioned lending are thus undermined and lose credibility with borrowers and lenders alike. Adding yet further conditions involving governance, according to this line of argument, would only exacerbate the problem of too many conditions.

There has undoubtedly been a problem of developed-country governments and international institutions attaching too many and sometimes contradictory conditions to their aid to African countries. The problem needs attention and could be dealt with in an ARC, where all public creditors and aid donors could be encouraged to better coordinate their aid to individual countries through a discussion and examination of their aid programs as well as the reform programs of the African participant. The specific problem of adding conditions involving governance to economic reform programs can be minimized if those conditions were made *ex ante* requirements for participation in an ARC. It is likely that some African governments, for example Ghana, would already qualify for an ARC. Backsliding on economic governance could, of course, result in the termination of an ARC.

To make an ARC work, creditor governments and international institutions would have to have the political will to sanction unacceptable economic performance on the part of an African participant by reducing aid and debt relief, as well as to reward good performance with more aid and debt relief. They would also have to be willing to criticize one another's programs when those have fallen short of commitments or have been inconsistent with agreed-upon reform and development strategies in an African ARC participant. In the past, a number of developed-country governments have deployed their aid in pursuit of interests (e.g., geopolitical or commercial interests) other than those associated with development in the country receiving the aid. But the decline in Africa's global importance, in both world economic and political terms, may now create an unusual opportunity for developed-country governments to tie their aid directly to development in Africa, and in particular to cooperate more effectively to promote and finance effective economic reforms.

It may also be objected that an ARC arrangement would be more intrusive in its potential impact on African government policies and behavior than present arrangements and that it would single out African governments for particularly stringent conditionalities. The ARC proposal is not intended to enlarge the number of conditionalities. Indeed, it is important, if an ARC is to function effectively, that the number of conditionalities be reduced to what is realistically manageable by the African government. It would attempt to ensure that conditionalities are consistent and are focused primarily on long-run development goals. What an ARC is intended to do is ensure that the reform programs supported by external creditors and aid donors are taken seriously both by the reforming government and by outside powers and institutions. An African government's failure to implement agreed reforms, or its reversal of such reforms (except where all parties agree in retrospect that implementation would have been unwise or beyond a government's ability) would be sanctioned.

The criticism that an ARC would single out African governments is a fair one. But the special treatment of participating governments is well justified for a number of reasons. The development problems of Africa are among the most extensive and pressing of any in the world, requiring a comprehensive, concentrated, and sustained attack on them, both by the African governments themselves and by external financing agencies. An ARC would provide the focus for that attack, by among other things placing a priority on adequate funding of reform programs through debt relief and aid, provided in a manner that would avoid undermining incentives for continuing reform efforts by the participating African government. For African countries, where domestic constituencies for reform are weak or nonexistent, an ARC would play a particularly important role in providing the external incentives and pressures needed to sustain reform programs.

An ARC would also promote coordination among external donors and creditors to ensure consistent and responsible behavior on the part of those governments and international institutions, while minimizing the burden on African economic managers of dealing with disparate and sometimes conflicting pressures for reform from abroad. Finally, by symbolizing to a world increasingly disillusioned about the seriousness of African leaders that they can put their own economic houses in order, an ARC can provide a measure of protection against the tendency, increasingly apparent among developed-country governments, to shift attention and concessional resources to the pursuit of other objectives in other parts of the world.

Further objections to the ARC proposal offered here might include, first, the likelihood of "contamination"—the danger that other debtor governments or US citizens with debts to the US government might claim that they deserve the same treatment being provided low-income Africans. There is no reason why an ARC arrangement could not be extended to low-income, debt-distressed countries outside Africa. At present, the World Bank includes only two non-African countries in this category: Guyana and Myanmar (Burma). Some of the poorer debt-distressed countries of Africa classified as middle-income, like Congo and Cote d'Ivoire, might also be included in an ARC program.

Another possible objection is that the proposal offered here might create a moral hazard—that debt relief for an African or any government that demonstrates an inability to service its debt might provide incentives for poor economic management or overborrowing and make debt problems worse in the future. This argument also appears unconvincing. Any external borrowing that most low-income African governments are likely to undertake in the foreseeable future will come largely from foreign governments and the IFIs. Those lenders will have a great deal to say about how much and for what purposes that borrowing is undertaken, and will share in the responsibility for its economic consequences. These are the same institutions that are pressing African governments to implement needed economic reforms, and so they can ensure consistency between their lending operations and the implementation and maintenance of reforms by African borrowers.

The problem of moral hazard should be easily controllable under these circumstances. Indeed, it has been argued that the real problem of moral hazard for highly indebted governments, with so much debt and so little hope of ever repaying it, is that their hopelessness might discourage serious efforts on their part to tackle their own economic problems. What has kept debt problems from undermining incentives for reform in Africa is the conditioning of additional aid and debt relief on continuing reforms. Further relief, properly handled, could provide additional incentives for reform.

The Role of Debt Relief

How much debt relief would this proposal offer low-income African countries? The initiative proposed here would cancel or concessionally reschedule all the bilateral public debt (concessional aid and export credits) scheduled to be serviced by an individual participating African government for the period covered by the ARC. In regard to debt servicing, if all 24 severely indebted low-income African countries had qualified for debt relief in an ARC arrangement in 1989, that relief would have produced a reduction of $800 million or 16 percent of their debt-servicing payments that year, reducing their average debt service ratio from 24 percent to 19 percent.

Since only the stock of bilateral public debt to be serviced during the two-year period covered by an ARC would be extinguished or rescheduled on highly concessional terms, the reduction in the debt stocks of ARC participants would be small in any given reform period. Over time, however, the reduction in the stock of debt could become quite substantial.

The ARC proposal does not include debt relief or rescheduling on the part of the IFIs, which now hold an increasing proportion of the stock of the debt and receive a growing proportion of the debt servicing of low-income African governments. However, if African borrowers do not achieve healthy growth rates over the coming decade, they may find it impossible to service their IFI debts, and relief from those debts may become necessary.

The proposal advanced here likewise does not address the private debt of low-income Africa. A portion of that debt consists of short-term trade credits, which, in contrast to long-term commercial lending, has not dried up for most low-income African countries, although for many it has become more costly (Brun and Goopta 1990). These short-term obligations continue to be serviced because the African borrowers do not wish to lose access to such credits in the future. In regard to long-term private credits, the Africans have several options. They can follow the example of Niger and negotiate deeply discounted buybacks, using World Bank funds and funds from other sources. This option should be attractive to commercial banks with loans outstanding in severely indebted, low-income African countries, since the abilities of the latter to service those debts are limited, and the likelihood is equally limited that banks will resume long-term commercial lending to them in the foreseeable future. Where there are no prospects of future lending or of full debt servicing, the banks should be encouraged to take advantage of opportunities to cash out. Alternatively, African participants in an

ARC could seek to reschedule their long-term commercial loans on the same concessional terms on which they would reschedule their public credits under an ARC (e.g., 40-year terms, 10 years grace, and nominal rates of interest).

Where buyback or rescheduling opportunities do not exist, either because banks are unwilling to participate or because African governments cannot afford to buy back the debts at market rates, Africans have the option of simply accumulating arrears on their commercial loans. The ARC arrangement would not make rescheduling or repayment of long-term commercial debt a precondition for participation. Nor would any low-income African country participating in an ARC be damaging its prospects for new lending, since commercial banks appear unwilling at present to make new credits available to them in any case. The commercial banks' financial health would be little affected, if at all, by such arrears, since loans to low-income African countries represent a relatively small proportion of their outstanding loans, and most banks have set aside reserves to cover losses from such loans.

5 The Role of the United States

Why should the United States provide aid or debt relief at all to the countries of sub-Saharan Africa? US economic interests in the region are minimal, US security interests have always been limited and have diminished further with the end of the Cold War, and US domestic pressures for support for these countries are far from compelling. The answer to this question must be that, for primarily humanitarian reasons—helping Africans make a better life for themselves—the United States should continue to provide a measure of assistance where it is needed and can be used effectively. Helping poor countries develop—even those countries where US economic and political interests are few—has been a part of US foreign policy during much of the postwar period and is likely to continue so into the future.

If constraints on foreign assistance continue to build in the future, the need and the pressures for debt relief in sub-Saharan Africa will continue as well. A number of proposals, including some made by the governments of the Group of Seven (G-7) countries, are already on the table. These proposals and others are likely to be put on the agenda of the economic summits, the annual meetings of the World Bank and the IMF, and other fora where issues of international debt and development are considered. Discussions of further debt relief raise the opportunity to address the broader issues of managing external support for reform in low-income Africa. The United States should be prepared to support further debt relief measures—for example, the Trinidad terms proposed by John Major—but it should do so in the context of a broader initiative for support of economic reform in low-income Africa.

To date, the United States has been the least forthcoming of the G-7 countries on debt relief for African countries. It was among the last to agree to debt cancellation, and it has opted for the least concessional approach to debt rescheduling under the Toronto menu approach (that is, the lengthening of maturities to 25 years rather than a reduction in the stock of debt or concessional interest rates). But pressures for more generous treatment of African debt will gain additional strength with recent US initiatives, namely, the cancellation of a large portion of Polish and Egyptian official debt and the Enterprise for the Americas initiative. These US initiatives are too many for the Bush administration to argue that they are special, non-precedent-setting cases.

Unlike the debts of the Egyptian and Latin American governments, the bilateral official debt owed to the United States by African countries is small, amounting to only $4.9 billion as of September 1990,[1] or roughly 4 percent of the total debt of these countries. Furthermore, the United States has only limited economic and political interests in sub-Saharan Africa. Domestic pressures for special aid or debt initiatives for Africa have been relatively weak. This pressure has come primarily from African-American groups, who, although African-Americans make up over 10 percent of the US population, have tended to focus their political attention and actions primarily on problems confronting them at home and on the problems of political and civil rights in South Africa, rather than on the general economic problems of sub-Saharan Africa as a whole.

Although these factors reduce the costs to the United States of debt relief for Africa, they also make it less likely that the US government will take the lead in pushing for more debt relief for the region. The proposals on further debt relief for Africa on the international table have been described in chapter 3. They represent two different approaches: adjustment of current practices, for example liberalizing the Toronto terms; and more sweeping action, such as outright cancellation or long-term moratoria on repayments. The first approach is a relatively low-cost, low-benefit one, for both debtor and creditor governments. And it continues to treat debt issues separately from overall resource and development issues in low-income Africa. Moreover, the Trinidad proposals, by reducing the entire stock of debt owed by low-income African governments (rather than the debt due during the consolidation period, as proposed in this study) would reduce the ability of creditors to reward African governments for implementing effective reform programs.

---

1. Data on the debt owed to the US government are drawn from Office of the Assistant Secretary for International Affairs (1990).

The second, more sweeping approach offers greater benefits to debtors and imposes greater costs on creditor governments. But many of these types of proposals would provide debt relief to all African governments indiscriminately. Even where these more generous approaches specify that only countries undertaking reforms would be eligible, they still treat debt relief separately from questions of overall resource needs, potentially compounding problems of coherence and consistency.

The United States is likely to want to avoid appearing to reject new proposals from its allies on African debt. Such a rejection could reinforce the perception at home (especially among African-Americans) that the administration is indifferent to African needs but willing to provide generous debt relief to a growing number of countries in other parts of the world where it has a major economic or political interest. This could complicate future efforts by the administration to persuade its allies to support debt relief for such countries. (This is not an imaginary problem. Despite US efforts at persuasion, the allies proved unwilling to adopt debt relief terms for Poland or Egypt as generous as those provided by the United States.)

To respond to African debt relief proposals likely to be tabled at upcoming international meetings, the United States as well as other G-7 governments with limited interests in Africa—for example, Japan and Germany—may want to develop their own African debt initiative along the lines of the one proposed in this study. Such proposals would exchange debt relief, and greater assurance of adequate levels of future concessional financing, for sustained implementation of economic reform programs.

The $4.9 billion in debt owed the US government by African countries in mid-1990 was made up of the following elements: $1.8 billion in Eximbank credits, $1 billion in foreign aid (development assistance and Economic Support Funds [ESF]), $1.6 billion in PL480 credits, and $500 million in military aid. By far the largest single sub-Saharan African debtor to the United States is Zaire, which owes a total of nearly $1.5 billion, just over $900 million of which is owed to the Eximbank. Sudan is the next largest debtor, owing $745 million. Nigeria is third with a debt of $648 million. Most of Sudan's debt is food aid and concessional economic assistance. Most of Nigeria's is owed to the Eximbank. In the Eximbank. In 1991, the United States canceled $728 million in concessional economic aid loans outstanding to African governments, $654 million of which was owed by governments of low-income, debt-distressed countries. The canceled debt consisted of principal and interest due during fiscal years 1990 through 1992.

An ARC initiative on African debt would be likely to involve further cancellation of debt-servicing payments on concessional loans (development assistance, ESF, and PL480) and the cancellation or concessional rescheduling of loans from the Eximbank and foreign military sales credits, thus reducing the debt servicing for countries participating in an ARC below what it would have been if they did not participate. As a result, revenues to the federal government would be lower than what they would have been in the absence of debt relief.

However, the amount of revenue reduction that would result from canceling even the entire debt of the low-income, debt-distressed African countries to the US government would not be great. If all of the countries in this group had participated in ARCs in 1989 and enjoyed complete relief from debt servicing for that year, the total reduction in US government revenue (from the *actual* amount expected rather than the amount scheduled to be paid) would have been less than $110 million. The budgetary costs to the United States and the savings in debt servicing to the African participants in an ARC program would not be great, but the savings from cancellations or debt servicing from other creditor governments could be substantial, as calculated in the previous chapter. Some in Washington would argue that this is a further reason for the US government to support additional debt relief for low-income Africa.

Legislation already exists, under section 572 of the Foreign Operations, Export Financing and Related Programs Appropriations Act, permitting the United States to cancel debts owed from development assistance and economic support funds. Besides this, the Food, Agriculture, Conservation and Trade Act of 1990, which contains legislation authorizing food aid programs, included an amendment (section 411) permitting a waiver of repayments of food aid loans for least developed countries with appropriate economic reform programs in place. Existing legislation does not permit the Eximbank to cancel debt owed it. However, one exception to this rule has already been legislated for Poland,

and another is in the works for Latin America. The precedent is set for further cancellation of Eximbank debt. In any case, there is nothing in Eximbank's legislation at present that prohibits it from rescheduling its loans on highly concessional terms, including below-market rates of interest.[2] Such reschedulings would not affect the nominal value of the loan but would reduce its discounted present value, and so reduce the present value of the debtor's stock of debt as well as the amount of debt servicing.

In considering further initiatives on debt reduction for the severely indebted countries of Africa, the recent initiatives of the Bush administration provide one clear lesson: where there is a political will, there is always a way—budgetary, legislative, and political obstacles notwithstanding. It can be done.

2. It has already rescheduled loans at rates of interest below those included in the original loan when current market rates of interest were lower than those carried by the loan.

Appendix: Statistical Tables

TABLE A.1 **Basic indicators for the 45 countries of sub-Saharan Africa, 1987**[a]

Country	Population (millions)	GNP per capita: Dollars	GNP per capita: Average annual growth rate (percentages) 1965–73	1973–80	1980–87	Life expectancy at birth (years)
Total	451.2	330	29.9	0.1	−2.8	51
Low-income economies	397.3	270	3.1	0.3	−3.6	50
Excluding Nigeria	290.6	240	0.8	−0.6	−2.2	50
Ethiopia	44.8	130	1.1	0.0	−1.6	47
Chad	5.3	150	−1.3	−3.5	2.4	46
Zaire	32.6	150	0.3	−4.7	−2.5	52
Guinea-Bissau	0.9	160	—	−4.2	0.8	39
Malawi	7.9	160	4.3	1.4	0.0	46
Mozambique	14.6	170	—	—	−8.2	48
Tanzania	23.9	180	2.0	−0.9	−1.7	53
Burkina Faso	8.3	190	1.2	2.5	2.5	47
Madagascar	10.9	210	1.1	−1.5	−3.7	54
Mali	7.8	210	—	4.3	0.7	47
The Gambia	0.8	220	1.7	0.2	0.8	43
Burundi	5.0	250	3.2	1.9	−0.2	49
Zambia	7.2	250	−0.5	−2.2	−5.6	53
Niger	6.8	260	−3.7	2.6	−4.9	45
Uganda	15.7	260	0.7	−6.2	−2.4	48

Sao Tome and Principe	0.1	280	—	7.2	−6.0	65
Somalia	5.7	290	−0.1	4.6	−2.5	47
Togo	3.2	290	2.0	1.5	−3.9	53
Rwanda	6.4	300	3.2	2.2	−1.0	49
Sierra Leone	3.8	300	2.3	−0.8	−2.0	41
Benin	4.3	310	0.0	−0.3	−0.6	50
Central African Republic	2.7	330	1.5	−0.5	−0.7	50
Kenya	22.1	330	4.7	1.3	−0.9	58
Sudan	23.1	330	−1.7	3.5	−4.3	50
Comoros	0.4	370	—	—	—	56
Lesotho	1.6	370	4.2	6.6	−0.9	56
Nigeria	106.6	370	5.3	1.2	−4.8	51
Ghana	13.6	390	1.0	−2.1	−2.0	54
Mauritania	1.9	440	1.2	−0.6	−1.6	46
Liberia	2.3	450	2.4	−0.7	−5.2	54
Equatorial Guinea	0.4	—	—	—	—	46
Guinea	6.5	—	1.2	1.3	−0.1	42
Middle-income economies	53.9	870	1.9	−1.2	0.3	53
Cape Verde	0.3	500	—	7.3	1.2	65
Senegal	7.0	520	−0.8	−0.5	0.1	48
Zimbabwe	9.0	580	2.6	−2.0	−1.3	58
Swaziland	0.7	700	5.8	0.3	1.2	55

Table continues next page

TABLE A.1 **Basic indicators for the 45 countries of sub-Saharan Africa, 1987**[a] *(continued)*

Country	Population (millions)	GNP per capita				Life expectancy at birth (years)
		Dollars	Average annual growth rate (percentages)			
			1965–73	1973–80	1980–87	
Cote d'Ivoire	11.1	740	4.5	1.2	−3.0	52
Congo	2.0	870	4.2	1.1	1.7	59
Cameroon	10.9	970	−0.4	5.7	4.5	56
Botswana	1.1	1,050	9.3	7.3	8.0	59
Mauritius	1.0	1,490	0.8	3.9	4.4	67
Gabon	1.1	2,700	4.9	−1.2	−3.5	52
Seychelles	0.1	3,120	2.6	4.5	1.3	70
Angola	9.2	—	1.1	−9.8	—	44
Djibouti	0.4	—	—	—	—	47

a. Summary measures include estimates for missing country data. The summary measures for GNP per capita and life expectancy are weighted by population.

Source: Adapted with permission from World Bank (1989).

TABLE A.2 Official development assistance to sub-Saharan Africa, 1984–88

Country	Millions of dollars					As a percentage of GNP (1988)
	1984	1985	1986	1987	1988	
Low-income economies						
Ethiopia	364	715	636	634	970	17.4
Chad	115	182	165	198	264	28.8
Zaire	312	325	448	627	580	9.0
Guinea-Bissau	n.a.	58	71	104	n.a.	72.5[a]
Malawi	158	113	198	280	366	30.6
Mozambique	259	300	422	651	886	70.6
Tanzania	558	487	681	882	978	31.2
Burkina Faso	189	198	284	281	298	16.0
Madagascar	153	188	316	321	305	16.2
Mali	321	380	372	366	427	22.0
The Gambia	n.a.	50	101	103	n.a.	58.6[a]
Burundi	141	142	187	202	187	17.1
Zambia	239	328	464	430	478	12.0
Niger	161	304	307	353	371	15.5
Uganda	163	182	198	279	359	8.4
Sao Tome and Principe	n.a.	12	12	18	n.a.	64.3[a]
Somalia	350	353	511	580	433	42.9
Togo	110	114	174	126	199	14.7
Rwanda	165	181	211	245	253	11.0

Table continued next page

TABLE A.2 Official development assistance to sub-Saharan Africa, 1984–88 *(continued)*

Country	Millions of dollars					As a percentage of GNP (1988)
	1984	1985	1986	1987	1988	
Sierra Leone	61	66	87	68	102	6.0[a]
Benin	77	95	138	138	162	9.0
Central African Republic	114	104	139	176	196	17.5
Kenya	411	438	455	572	808	9.4
Sudan	622	1,128	945	898	918	7.8
Comoros	n.a.	47	46	53	n.a.	35.9[a]
Lesotho	101	94	88	107	108	26.3
Nigeria	33	32	59	69	120	0.4
Ghana	216	203	371	373	474	9.1
Mauritania	175	209	225	182	184	18.4
Liberia	133	90	97	78	65	n.a.
Equatorial Guinea	n.a.	17	22	42	n.a.	n.a.
Guinea	123	119	175	213	262	10.3
Middle-income economies						
Cape Verde	n.a.	70	109	86	n.a.	57.4[a]
Senegal	368	295	567	641	568	11.4
Zimbabwe	298	237	225	294	273	4.3
Swaziland	n.a.	25	35	45	n.a.	9.1[a]
Cote d'Ivoire	128	125	186	254	439	4.5

Congo	98	71	110	152	89	4.1
Cameroon	186	159	224	213	284	2.2
Botswana	102	96	102	156	151	7.8
Mauritius	36	28	56	65	59	3.0
Gabon	76	61	79	82	106	3.2
Seychelles	n.a	22	28	24	n.a	7.7[a]
Djibouti	n.a	81	115	92	n.a	n.a

n.a. = not available.
a. Figures are for 1987
Source: Adapted with permission from World Bank (1990b, 216–17, table 20) and World Bank (1989, 251, table 18).

TABLE A.3 External debt of sub-Saharan Africa, 1985 and 1989

	1985			1989		
Country	Total debt (millions of dollars)	Debt-GNP ratio	Debt service ratio	Total debt (millions of dollars	Debt-GNP ratio	Debt service ratio
Low-income economies						
Ethiopia	1,869	39.4	26.7	3,013	50.6	38.7
Chad	186	25.7	17.2	368	36.7	5.2
Zaire	6,027	88.8	25.7	8,843	96.6	21.5
Guinea-Bissau	304	194.9	48.0	458	274.3	42.9
Malawi	1,018	94.1	38.9	1,394	89.4	28.0
Mozambique	2,863	87.4	31.6	4,737	474.2	24.4
Tanzania	3,867	56.8	22.5	4,918	186.1	16.6
Burkina Faso	535	37.4	10.1	756	26.9	9.4
Madagascar	2,460	89.0	42.8	3,607	154.1	52.4
Mali	1,468	141.2	17.5	2,157	105.3	18.6
The Gambia	245	166.6	10.4	342	172.9	10.9
Burundi	446	39.2	19.3	867	81.9	32.8
Zambia	4,639	229.4	16.0	6,874	137.9	12.3
Niger	1,208	80.6	39.0	1,578	79.4	33.0
Uganda	1,171	39.8	43.1	1,808	44.7	81.2
Sao Tome and Principe	62	187.0	29.1	131	329.7	44.7
Somalia	1,639	197.8	15.7	2,137	202.8	34.0
Togo	937	129.1	27.3	1,185	91.8	18.8

Rwanda	369	21.6	10.4	652	30.2	18.5
Sierra Leone	724	48.7	12.5	1,057	118.9	n.a.
Benin	812	75.0	16.2	1,177	71.9	6.6
Central African Republic	348	50.2	14.2	716	65.8	14.3
Kenya	4,309	72.9	41.9	5,690	71.7	33.3
Sudan	9,127	143.7	12.0	12,965	82.9	7.9
Comoros	133	116.9	9.2	176	88.2	9.2
Lesotho	173	35.8	6.7	324	39.0	2.8
Nigeria	19,551	22.2	33.3	32,832	119.3	21.3
Ghana	2,174	49.1	24.0	3,078	59.9	42.2
Mauritania	1,502	225.8	25.3	2,010	213.2	20.1
Liberia	1,247	121.0	8.6	1,761	n.a.	n.a.
Equatorial Guinea	132	172.0	41.6	228	182.7	18.7
Guinea	1,438	n.a.	n.a.	2,176	85.3	15.2
Middle-income economies						
Cape Verde	97	72.0	n.a.	130	45.9	n.a.
Senegal	2,559	105.9	22.2	4,139	93.2	29.4
Zimbabwe	2,465	59.0	28.4	3,088	53.6	25.6
Swaziland	238	63.7	9.4	281	43.6	4.8
Cote d'Ivoire	9,746	154.6	44.7	15,412	182.2	40.9
Congo	3,033	157.0	34.0	4,316	214.9	27.0
Cameroon	2,940	38.5	22.7	4,734	42.2	19.4
Botswana	334	37.9	4.2	513	38.5[a]	3.6

Table continues next page

TABLE A.3 External debt of sub-Saharan Africa, 1985 and 1989 *(continued)*

Country	1985			1989		
	Total debt (millions of dollars)	Debt-GNP ratio	Debt service ratio	Total debt (millions of dollars	Debt-GNP ratio	Debt service ratio
Mauritius	629	61.0	24.2	832	41.0	9.8
Gabon	1,207	39.1	11.6	3,176	108.9	11.9
Seychelles	98	74.0	9.0	168	60.4	11.9
Djibouti	144	41.2	4.3	180	n.a.	n.a.

n.a. = not available.
a. Figure is for 1988.
Source: World Bank (1990a, vol. 2).

References

Agency for International Development. 1990. *The Democracy Initiative*. Washington: AID (December).

Agency for International Development. 1991. *Congressional Presentation*. Washington: AID.

Berg, Elliot. 1990. *Adjustment Postponed: Economic Policy Reform in Senegal in the 1980s*. Report for AID (October).

Brun, Richard, and Sudarshan Goopta. 1990. "The Role and Cost of Short-term Trade Credit." Paper presented at the Symposium on African External Finance in the 1990s, Washington (September).

Calleghy, Thomas. 1990. "Lost Between State and Market: The Politics of Economic Adjustment in Ghana, Zambia and Nigeria." In Joan Nelson, ed., *Economic Crisis and Policy Choice*. Princeton: Princeton University Press.

Chang, P. H. Kevin, and Robert E. Cumby. 1990. "Capital Flight in Sub-Saharan African Countries." Paper presented to a World Bank symposium on African External Finance, Washington (September).

Culagovsky, Jorge, Victor Gabor, Maria Cristina Germany, and Charles P. Humphreys. 1991. "African Financing Needs in the 1990s." *PRE Working Paper*. Washington: World Bank (forthcoming).

Demirguc-Kunt, Asli, and Refik Erzan. 1991. "The Role of Officially Supported Export Credits in Sub-Saharan Africa's External Financing." *International Economics Department Working Paper* 603. Washington: World Bank (February).

Development Assistance Committee. 1990. *Development Cooperation: 1990 Report*. Paris: Organization for Economic Cooperation and Development.

Economic Commission for Africa. 1989. *African Alternative Framework for Structural Adjustment Programmes for Socio-Economic Recovery and Transformation*. New York: United Nations.

Eichengreen, Barry, and Peter H. Lindert. 1989. *The International Debt Crisis in Historical Perspective*. Cambridge, MA: MIT Press.

Green, Joshua. 1989. "The External Debt Problem of Sub-Saharan Africa." *Staff Papers* 36, no. 4 (December). Washington: International Monetary Fund.

Gulhati, Ravi. 1989a. *Impasse in Zambia: The Economics and Politics of Reform*. Washington: Economic Development Institute of the World Bank.

Gulhati, Ravi. 1989b. *Malawi: Promising Reforms, Bad Luck*. Washington: World Bank.

Helleiner, Gerald. 1991. "The IMF, the World Bank and Africa's Adjustment and External Debt Problems: An Unofficial View." Paper presented to a symposium on Structural Adjustment, External Debt and Growth in Africa, sponsored by the Association of African Central Banks, Gaborone, Botswana (February).

Hermes, Niels, and Robert Lensink. 1990. "The Magnitudes and Determinants of Capital Flight: The Case for Six Sub-Saharan Countries." Groningen, the Netherlands: University of Groningen (September, mimeographed).

Lancaster, Carol. 1991. "The New Politics of US Aid to Africa." *Africa Notes* 120 (28 January). Washington: Center for Strategic and International Studies.

McPherson, Malcolm, and Steven Radelet. 1989. "Economic Reform in the Gambia: Politics, Politics, Foreign Aid and Luck." *Development Discussion Paper* 300. Cambridge, MA: Harvard Institute for International Development (June).

Nkrumah, Kwame. 1970. *Ghana: The Autobiography of Kwame Nkrumah*. New York: International Publications.

Nowels, Larry. 1991. *Egyptian Military Debt Forgiveness: Costs, Implications, and the Role of Congress*. Washington: Congressional Research Service (31 January).

Office of the Assistant Secretary for International Affairs. 1990. *Status of Active Foreign Credits of the United States Government*. Washington: Treasury Department (30 September).

Rieffel, Alexis. 1984. "The Paris Club, 1978–83." *Columbia Journal of Transnational Law* 23, no. 1.

Rieffel, Alexis. 1985. "The Role of the Paris Club in Managing Debt Problems." *Essays in International Finance* 161. Princeton: Princeton University (December).

Serafino, Nina, and Betsy Cody. 1991. *The Enterprise for the Americas Initiative: Issues for Congress*. Washington: Congressional Research Service (21 February).

van de Walle, Etienne, and Andrew Foster. 1990. "Fertility Decline in Africa." *World Bank Technical Paper* 125. Washington: World Bank.

Williamson, John. 1990. *The Progress of Policy Reform in Latin America*. POLICY ANALYSES IN INTERNATIONAL ECONOMICS 28. Washington: Institute for International Economics.

Williamson, John. 1991. Equilibrium Exchange Rates: An Update. POLICY ANALYSES IN INTERNATIONAL ECONOMICS 35. Washington: Institute for International Economics.

World Bank. 1981. *Accelerated Development in Sub-Saharan Africa*. Washington: World Bank.

World Bank. 1988. *Rural Development: World Bank Experience 1965–86*. Washington: World Bank.

World Bank. 1989. *Sub-Saharan Africa: From Crisis to Sustainable Growth*. Washington: World Bank.

World Bank. 1990a. *World Debt Tables 1990–91*. Washington: World Bank.

World Bank. 1990b. *World Development Report*. Washington: World Bank.

World Bank. 1990c. *Special Program of Assistance: Growth, Aid, Debt: Proposal for the Second Phase*. Washington: World Bank Africa Region (July).

World Bank. 1990d. *Evaluation Results for 1988*. Washington: World Bank.

POLICY ANALYSES IN INTERNATIONAL ECONOMICS

1 **The Lending Policies of the International Monetary Fund**
John Williamson/*August 1982*
$8.00 ISBN 0-88132-000-5 72 pp

2 **"Reciprocity": A New Approach to World Trade Policy?**
William R. Cline/*September 1982*
$8.00 ISBN 0-88132-001-3 41 pp

3 **Trade Policy in the 1980s**
C. Fred Bergsten and William R. Cline/*November 1982*
(Out of print) ISBN 0-88132-002-1 84 pp
Partially reproduced in the book *Trade Policy in the 1980s.*

4 **International Debt and the Stability of the World Economy**
William R. Cline/*September 1983*
$10.00 ISBN 0-88132-010-2 134 pp

5 **The Exchange Rate System, Second Edition**
John Williamson/*September 1983, rev. June 1985*
$10.00 ISBN 0-88132-034-X 61 pp

6 **Economic Sanctions in Support of Foreign Policy Goals**
Gary Clyde Hufbauer and Jeffrey J. Schott/*October 1983*
$10.00 ISBN 0-88132-014-5 109 pp

7 **A New SDR Allocation?**
John Williamson/*March 1984*
$10.00 ISBN 0-88132-028-5 61 pp

8 **An International Standard for Monetary Stabilization**
Ronald I. McKinnon/*March 1984*
$10.00 ISBN 0-88132-018-8 108 pp

9 **The Yen/Dollar Agreement: Liberalizing Japanese Capital Markets**
Jeffrey A. Frankel/*December 1984*
$10.00 ISBN 0-88132-035-8 86 pp

10 **Bank Lending to Developing Countries: The Policy Alternatives**
C. Fred Bergsten, William R. Cline, and John Williamson/*April 1985*
$12.00 ISBN 0-88132-032-3 221 pp

11 **Trading for Growth: The Next Round of Trade Negotiations**
Gary Clyde Hufbauer and Jeffrey J. Schott/*September 1985*
$10.00 ISBN 0-88132-033-1 109 pp

12 **Financial Intermediation Beyond the Debt Crisis**
Donald R. Lessard and John Williamson/*September 1985*
$12.00 ISBN 0-88132-021-8 130 pp

13 **The United States-Japan Economic Problem**
C. Fred Bergsten and William R. Cline/*October 1985, 2d ed. rev. January 1987*
$10.00 ISBN 0-88132-060-9 180 pp

14 **Deficits and the Dollar: The World Economy at Risk**
Stephen Marris/*December 1985, 2d ed. rev. November 1987*
$18.00 ISBN 0-88132-067-6 415 pp

15 **Trade Policy for Troubled Industries**
Gary Clyde Hufbauer and Howard F. Rosen/*March 1986*
$10.00 ISBN 0-88132-020-X 111 pp

16 **The United States and Canada: The Quest for Free Trade**
Paul Wonnacott, with an Appendix by John Williamson/*March 1987*
$10.00 ISBN 0-88132-056-0 188 pp

17 **Adjusting to Success: Balance of Payments Policy in the East Asian NICs,** revised edition
Bela Balassa and John Williamson/*June 1987, rev. April 1990*
$11.95 ISBN 0-88132-101-X 160 pp

18 **Mobilizing Bank Lending to Debtor Countries**
William R. Cline/*June 1987*
$10.00 ISBN 0-88132-062-5 100 pp

19 **Auction Quotas and United States Trade Policy**
C. Fred Bergsten, Kimberly Ann Elliott, Jeffrey J. Schott, and Wendy E. Takacs/*September 1987*
$10.00 ISBN 0-88132-050-1 254 pp

20 **Agriculture and the GATT: Rewriting the Rules**
Dale E. Hathaway/*September 1987*
$10.00 ISBN 0-88132-052-8 169 pp

21 **Anti-Protection: Changing Forces in United States Trade Politics**
I. M. Destler and John S. Odell/*September 1987*
$10.00 ISBN 0-88132-043-9 220 pp

22 **Targets and Indicators: A Blueprint for the International Coordination of Economic Policy**
John Williamson and Marcus H. Miller/*September 1987*
$10.00 ISBN 0-88132-051-X 118 pp

23 **Capital Flight: The Problem and Policy Responses**
Donald R. Lessard and John Williamson/*December 1987*
$10.00 ISBN 0-88132-059-5 80 pp

24 **United States-Canada Free Trade: An Evaluation of the Agreement**
Jeffrey J. Schott/*April 1988*
$3.95 ISBN 0-88132-072-2 48 pp

25 **Voluntary Approaches to Debt Relief**
John Williamson/*September 1988, rev. May 1989*
$10.95 ISBN 0-88132-075-7 80 pp

26 **American Trade Adjustment: The Global Impact**
William R. Cline/*March 1989*
$12.95 ISBN 0-88132-095-1 98 pp

27 **More Free Trade Areas?**
Jeffrey J. Schott/*May 1989*
$10.00 ISBN 0-88132-085-4 88 pp

28 **The Progress of Policy Reform in Latin America**
John Williamson/*January 1990*
$10.95 ISBN 0-88132-100-1 106 pp

29 **The Global Trade Negotiations: What Can Be Achieved?**
Jeffrey J. Schott/*September 1990*
$10.95 ISBN 0-88132-137-0 72 pp

30 **Economic Policy Coordination: Requiem or Prologue?**
Wendy Dobson/*April 1991*
$11.95 ISBN 0-88132-102-8 162 pp

31 **The Economic Opening of Eastern Europe**
John Williamson/*May 1991*
$11.95 ISBN 0-88132-186-9 92 pp

32 **Eastern Europe and the Soviet Union in the World Economy**
Susan M. Collins and Dani Rodrik/*May 1991*
$12.95 ISBN 0-88132-157-5 172 pp

33 **African Economic Reform: The External Dimension**
Carol Lancaster/*June 1991*
$12.95 ISBN 0-88132-096-X 80 pp

BOOKS

IMF Conditionality
John Williamson, editor/*1983*
$35.00 (cloth only) ISBN 0-88132-006-4 695 pp

Trade Policy in the 1980s
William R. Cline, editor/*1983*
$35.00 (cloth) ISBN 0-88132-008-1 810 pp
$20.00 (paper) ISBN 0-88132-031-5 810 pp

Subsidies in International Trade
Gary Clyde Hufbauer and Joanna Shelton Erb/*1984*
$35.00 (cloth only) ISBN 0-88132-004-8 299 pp

International Debt: Systemic Risk and Policy Response
William R. Cline/*1984*
$30.00 (cloth only) ISBN 0-88132-015-3 336 pp

Trade Protection in the United States: 31 Case Studies
Gary Clyde Hufbauer, Diane E. Berliner, and Kimberly Ann Elliott/*1986*
$25.00 ISBN 0-88132-040-4 371 pp

Toward Renewed Economic Growth in Latin America
Bela Balassa, Gerardo M. Bueno, Pedro-Pablo Kuczynski, and Mario Henrique Simonsen/*1986*
$15.00 ISBN 0-88132-045-5 205 pp

American Trade Politics: System Under Stress
I. M. Destler/*1986*
$30.00 (cloth) ISBN 0-88132-058-7 380 pp
$18.00 (paper) ISBN 0-88132-057-9 380 pp

The Future of World Trade in Textiles and Apparel
William R. Cline/*1987, rev. June 1990*
$20.00 ISBN 0-88132-110-9 344 pp

Capital Flight and Third World Debt
Donald R. Lessard and John Williamson, editors/*1987*
$16.00 ISBN 0-88132-053-6 270 pp

The Canada-United States Free Trade Agreement: The Global Impact
Jeffrey J. Schott and Murray G. Smith, editors/*1988*
$13.95 ISBN 0-88132-073-0 211 pp

Managing the Dollar: From the Plaza to the Louvre
Yoichi Funabashi/*1988, rev. 1989*
$19.95 ISBN 0-88132-097-8 307 pp

World Agricultural Trade: Building a Consensus
William M. Miner and Dale E. Hathaway, editors/*1988*
$16.95 ISBN 0-88132-071-3 226 pp

Japan in the World Economy
Bela Balassa and Marcus Noland/*1988*
$19.95 ISBN 0-88132-041-2 306 pp

America in the World Economy: A Strategy for the 1990s
C. Fred Bergsten/*1988*
$29.95 (cloth) ISBN 0-88132-089-7 235 pp
$13.95 (paper) ISBN 0-88132-082-X 235 pp

United States External Adjustment and the World Economy
William R. Cline/*May 1989*
$25.00 ISBN 0-88132-048-X 392 pp

Free Trade Areas and U.S. Trade Policy
Jeffrey J. Schott, editor/*May 1989*
$19.95 ISBN 0-88132-094-3 400 pp

Dollar Politics: Exchange Rate Policymaking in the United States
I. M. Destler and C. Randall Henning/*September 1989*
$11.95 ISBN 0-88132-079-X 192 pp

Foreign Direct Investment in the United States
Edward M. Graham and Paul R. Krugman/*December 1989*
$11.95 ISBN 0-88132-074-9 161 pp

Latin American Adjustment: How Much Has Happened?
John Williamson, editor/*April 1990*
$34.95 ISBN 0-88132-125-7 480 pp

Completing the Uruguay Round: A Results-Oriented Approach to the GATT Trade Negotiations/*September 1990*
Jeffrey J. Schott, editor
$19.95 ISBN 0-88132-130-3 256 pp

Economic Sanctions Reconsidered (in two volumes)
History and Current Policy (also sold separately, see below)
Supplemental Case Histories
Gary Clyde Hufbauer, Jeffrey J. Schott, and Kimberly Ann Elliott/
1985, 2d ed. December 1990
$65.00 (cloth) ISBN 0-88132-015-X 928 pp
$45.00 (paper) ISBN 0-88132-105-2 928 pp

Economic Sanctions Reconsidered: History and Current Policy
Gary Clyde Hufbauer, Jeffrey J. Schott, and Kimberly Ann Elliott/
2d ed. December 1990
$36.00 (cloth) ISBN 0-88132-136-2 288 pp
$25.00 (paper) ISBN 0-88132-140-0 288 pp

Pacific Basin Developing Countries: Prospects for the Future
Marcus Noland/*January 1991*
$29.95 (cloth) ISBN 0-88132-141-9 250 pp
$19.95 (paper) ISBN 0-88132-081-1 250 pp

SPECIAL REPORTS

1 **Promoting World Recovery: A Statement on Global Economic Strategy**
by Twenty-six Economists from Fourteen Countries/*December 1982*
(Out of print) ISBN 0-88132-013-7 45 pp

2 **Prospects for Adjustment in Argentina, Brazil, and Mexico: Responding to the Debt Crisis**
John Williamson, editor/*June 1983*
(Out of print) ISBN 0-88132-016-1 71 pp

3 **Inflation and Indexation: Argentina, Brazil, and Israel**
John Williamson, editor/*March 1985*
(Out of print) ISBN 0-88132-037-4 191 pp

4 **Global Economic Imbalances**
C. Fred Bergsten, editor/*March 1986*
$25.00 (cloth) ISBN 0-88132-038-2 126 pp
$10.00 (paper) ISBN 0-88132-042-0 126 pp

5 **African Debt and Financing**
Carol Lancaster and John Williamson, editors/*May 1986*
$12.00 ISBN 0-88132-044-7 229 pp

6 **Resolving the Global Economic Crisis: After Wall Street**
Thirty-three Economists from Thirteen Countries/*December 1987*
$3.00 ISBN 0-88132-070-6 30 pp

7 **World Economic Problems**
Kimberly Ann Elliott and John Williamson, editors/*April 1988*
$15.95 ISBN 0-88132-055-2 298 pp

Reforming World Agricultural Trade
Twenty-nine Professionals from Seventeen Countries/*1988*
$3.95 ISBN 0-88132-088-9 42 pp

8 **Economic Relations Between the United States and Korea: Conflict or Cooperation?**
Thomas O. Bayard and Soo-Gil Young, editors/*January 1989*
$12.95 ISBN 0-88132-068-4 192 pp

FORTHCOMING

Equilibrium Exchange Rates: An Update
John Williamson

Currency Convertibility in Eastern Europe
John Williamson

Managed and Mismanaged Trade: Policy Lessons for the 1990s
Laura D'Andrea Tyson

Korea in the World Economy
Il SaKong

The Dynamics of the Korean Development Model
Soon Cho

International Adjustment and Finance: The Lessons of 1985–1990
C. Fred Bergsten, editor

Has the Adjustment Process Worked?
Paul R. Krugman

Global Oil Crisis Intervention
Philip K. Verleger, Jr.

U.S. Taxation of International Income: Blueprint for Reform
Gary Clyde Hufbauer

Narrowing the U.S. Current Account Deficit: A Sectoral Assessment
Allen J. Lenz

Prospects for North American Free Trade
Jeffrey J. Schott and Gary Clyde Hufbauer

The United States as a Debtor Country
C. Fred Bergsten and Shafiqul Islam

The Effects of Foreign-Exchange Intervention
Kathryn Dominguez and Jeffrey A. Frankel

Sizing up U.S. Export Disincentives
J. David Richardson

Trading for the Environment
John Whalley

The Greenhouse Effect: Global Economic Consequences
William R. Cline

Energy Policy for the 1990s: A Global Perspective
Philip K. Verleger, Jr.

International Monetary Policymaking in the United States, Germany, and Japan
C. Randall Henning

The Future of the World Trading System
John Whalley

The New Tripolar World Economy: Toward Collective Leadership
C. Fred Bergsten and C. Randall Henning

The United States and Japan in the 1990s
C. Fred Bergsten, Marcus Noland and I. M. Destler

The Outlook for World Commodity Prices
Philip K. Verleger, Jr.

Reciprocity and Retaliation: An Evaluation of Aggressive Trade Policies
Thomas O. Bayard

Third World Debt: A Reappraisal
William R. Cline

The Costs of U.S. Trade Barriers
Gary Clyde Hufbauer and Kimberly Ann Elliott

A World Savings Shortage?
Paul R. Krugman

The Globalization of Industry and National Governments
C. Fred Bergsten and Edward M. Graham

Comparing the Costs of Protection: Europe, Japan, and the United States
Gary Clyde Hufbauer and Kimberly Ann Elliott, editors

Toward Freer Trade in the Western Hemisphere
Gary Clyde Hufbauer and Jeffrey J. Schott